THE LAWYER'S GUIDE TO Microsoft® OUTLOOK 2007

BEN M. SCHORR

ABA LAWPRACTICEMANAGEMENTSECTION
MARKETING • MANAGEMENT • TECHNOLOGY • FINANCE

Commitment to Quality: The Law Practice Management Section is committed to quality in our publications. Our authors are experienced practitioners in their fields. Prior to publication, the contents of all our books are rigorously reviewed by experts to ensure the highest quality product and presentation. Because we are committed to serving our readers' needs, we welcome your feedback on how we can improve future editions of this book.

Microsoft is a registered trademark of the Microsoft Corporation.

Cover design by Jim Colao.

Library of Congress Cataloging-in-Publication Data

Schorr, Ben M.
   Outlook 2007 for lawyers / Ben M. Schorr, Law Practice Management Section, American Bar Association.—1st ed.
      p. cm.
   Includes bibliographical references and index.
   ISBN 978-1-60442-143-9 (alk. paper)
   1. Law offices—United States—Automation. 2. Microsoft Outlook. 3. Legal correspondence—United States—Automation. 4. Electronic mail systems. 5. Personal information management—Computer programs. I. American Bar Association. Section of Law Practice Management. II. Title.

   KF320.A9S366 2008
   005.5'7024340092—dc22

                                                           2008022242

Dedication

To my grandparents, Keith and Helen Amstutz. Their generosity, wisdom, and genuine goodness has been a ceaseless inspiration to me.

Contents

Chapter 2
E-mail   23

Chapter 3
Handling To-Dos   63

Chapter 4
Calendaring   87

Chapter 5
Managing Your Contacts   103

Chapter 10
Troubleshooting   183

Chapter 11
Mistakes Lawyers Make with Outlook 197

Chapter 12
Tricks to Impress Your Law School Classmates 203

Chapter 13
Keyboard Shortcuts to Make You Smile 215

Acknowledgments

I'd like to give some special recognition to the following people:

My parents, Morry and Sharon Schorr, for their constant support, patience, humor, and the considerable genetic advantage.

The Outlook MVPs, in particular Vince Averello, Sue Mosher, Diane Poremsky, Milly Staples, Neo, Dmitry Streblechenko, Ken Slovak, Jessie Louise, Russ Valentine, and all the rest for their knowledge and friendship over the years. I'd be remiss if I didn't add Exchange MVPs Jim McBee and Chris Scharff, each of whom have been my writing partners in the past, to this list.

At Microsoft, Jensen Harris, KC Lemson, Ronna Pinkerton, Jeff Stephenson, and the Microsoft Outlook team in Redmond for being terrific and accessible and giving so much of their time to help me understand how the product works.

Patricia Eddy for being a voice of sanity and a dear friend when I desperately need both (on a nearly daily basis).

Jana Carter, who has just flashed a magical smile at seeing her name mentioned here, for confessions, questions, and for being such a vibrant and compelling soul. Nothing worthwhile is easy.

Paula Kingsley for throwing open the metaphorical curtains and letting the sun shine in again.

Jill Radke for helping to make something that could have been awful relatively painless and being a friend throughout.

Aaron Shumway and Mark Valencia (attorneys and gentlemen) for being my sounding boards and offering lots of valuable input on how attorneys really use this stuff.

My business partner, Matti Raihala, and the rest of the Roland Schorr & Tower team for keeping things running smoothly so I could spend all this time banging out this book.

And Sharon Nelson and John Simek for their support and friendship. This book never would have happened if it wasn't for Sharon's ceaseless willingness to help out.

About the Author

Ben M. Schorr is a technologist and Chief Executive Officer for Roland Schorr & Tower, a professional consulting firm head-quartered in Honolulu, Hawaii. In that capacity he consults with a wide variety of organizations including many law firms. He is frequently sought as a writer, teacher, and speaker for groups as diverse as the Hawaii Visitor and Convention Bureau and the American Bar Association. More than eleven years ago Microsoft named Mr. Schorr as an MVP in their Outlook prod-uct group, and he has been supporting Outlook, Exchange, and most recently OneNote ever since. Prior to co-founding Roland Schorr, he was the Director of Information Services for Damon Key Leong Kupchak Hastert, a large Honolulu law firm, for almost eight years.

Mr. Schorr was a contributing author for *Using Micro-soft Office 2000* by Que and has been a technical editor or contributor on a number of other books over the years. For several years he was half of the "Ask the Exchange Pros" team for Windows Server System magazine. He is the author of the forthcoming *The Lawyer's Guide to Microsoft Word 2007,* which is being published by the American Bar Association.

In October of 2005 Mr. Schorr was named by the Pacific. Technology Foundation as one of the Top 50 Technology Lead-ers in Hawaii. He is a member of the Institute of Electrical and Electronics Engineers' (IEEE) Computer Society, the American Bar Association, and the United States Naval Institute. In his free time Mr. Schorr enjoys coaching football, running mara-thons, reading, playing softball, and kayaking in the ocean, and he has completed the Tinman triathlon three times. His dog is not impressed. You can reach him at bens@rolandschorr .com.

Introduction

When I first sat down to start writing this book, I asked myself the key question:

> What is my message? What do I want the readers to get out of this book, and how can I make it truly compelling and useful?

OK, so maybe that's three questions. Anyhow, the answers to these questions are something I spent a lot of time thinking about and considering. The quick answer to all three questions is pretty clear: Most lawyers use Outlook and most lawyers use only a tiny bit of its power. With this book I want to help you get the most out of Microsoft Outlook in order to make you more effective, more efficient, and more successful. I'm hoping you find this book useful, powerful, and maybe even a little enjoyable.

We only use about 10% of our brains. If we could just figure out a way to use the other 80%, imagine what we could accomplish!

—Ellen Degeneres

To accomplish that, I'm going to tell you about Outlook through my eyes—the eyes of a ten-year veteran of Microsoft Outlook who is also a twenty-year veteran of law office technology. I'm hoping that you'll keep turning the pages because every new page will bring a series of moments: "Gee whiz" moments, "Holy cow!" moments, and "Lightbulb" moments. Hopefully, you'll put this book down repeatedly as you rush to your computer to try a new trick. If this book ends up on your desk with a colorful array of sticky notes protruding from the pages, then I'll know I've succeeded.

Why E-mail Matters

This almost seems like it shouldn't need any explanation, but e-mail has increasingly become the most popular method for business, and even personal, communication. Fax volume has declined precipitously as e-mail has replaced faxing as the preferred method for sending documents. E-mail is convenient, asynchronous, effective, inexpensive, and accessible. Even my grandparents have e-mail and know how to use it. Your clients, coworkers, co-counsel, experts, opposing counsel, and even the courts are all using e-mail all day, every day. Outlook, the Microsoft Office e-mail client, is the application that Microsoft Office users have open on their computers more than any other program in the suite. (How do we know that? Keep reading.)

Asynchronous?

E-mail is an asynchronous method of communication. That means that the two parties don't have to communicate with each other at the same time. I can send you an e-mail, and you can read it three hours from now and reply tomorrow. A telephone is an example of synchronous communication. Unless you reach an automated attendant, then nobody is communicating.

If you want to practice law today, you need to effectively utilize and manage e-mail. Probably a *lot* of e-mail. In fact, you probably have to manage so much e-mail that you are nearly getting buried by it. In this book I'm going to offer you some tips and tricks for effectively managing large volumes of e-mail.

What's Outlook?

Microsoft Outlook is Microsoft's personal information manager (PIM) software as well as its premier e-mail client. Although most people only think about the e-mail capabilities of the program—which maps nicely to how most people seem to prioritize their software usage these days—Outlook is also a very capable task, contact, and calendar manager. You can use it to manage your schedule and the schedule of a team of others. You can use Outlook for task management. You can use Outlook to log and track phone calls, meetings, and correspondence. You can use Outlook to manage a list of contacts and to initiate merges with Microsoft Word to create "personalized" letters or other documents.

Outlook is a lot more than just e-mail, and in this book we're going to try to help you get the most out of it so you can practice more effectively.

Those Who Love Software or the Law Should Not Watch Either Being Made

I thought an exploration of how the Office 2007 suite was made would be enlightening here. The story really begins with Office 2003. When you installed Office 2003, a funny little icon was added to the system tray (down on the task bar, next to the clock) where it sat, mysteriously staring at you. Eventually you clicked on it and when you did, a dialog box was presented that offered to let you opt-in to something called the Customer Experience Improvement Program. The Customer Experience Improvement Program (CEIP) sends a lot of non-identifiable data about how you actually use their software back to Microsoft. Don't worry, it doesn't send any actual documents or e-mail addresses or anything like that. Instead it's primarily concerned with *how* you use the software—what buttons you click, how many documents you have open, how many subfolders you create, and how long you spend in each program (that's how we know that Outlook stays open longer than any other Office application). Microsoft collects this data (known internally at Microsoft as "SQM" or "Service Quality Monitoring" data) to use as input when making the next version of Microsoft Office.

> Designing Microsoft Office is like ordering pizza for 400 million people.
>
> —Steven Sinofsky, Microsoft

Prior to the CEIP, boxes of dry erase markers were used in brainstorming sessions. Huge quantities of Chinese food were consumed behind one-way mirrors in the usability labs,

The most commonly clicked toolbar button in Microsoft Word 2003, and it's not even close, is "Paste," followed, in order, by "Save," "Copy," "Undo," and "Bold."

and survey after survey after survey was analyzed, all in the name of trying to figure out how users actually used the products. The results of all of that work became Office XP. Clearly a better way was needed, and the CEIP is it. Microsoft receives a mind-boggling volume of data from the CEIP; in fact, as of April 2006, it had received more than 1.3 *billion* sessions of Office 2003 usage. That data taught Microsoft a lot of interesting, useful, and surprising lessons and was of tremendous help in designing Microsoft Office 2007. As a result, Office 2007 is the first version of Office that was really built with volumes of direct feedback from real end users in real-life situations.

The ribbon in Microsoft Office makes it easier to find and use the features you want.

The results of that feedback can be seen in several areas, most notably the user interface (UI) where the old "File, Edit, View" menu structure has been largely (though not yet entirely) replaced with what is called "The Ribbon." When you first fire up Outlook 2007, you're going to wonder what I'm talking about because the File, Edit, View menu is still clearly in evidence. But click the button to start a new Mail item, and you'll see what I mean. The ribbon is intended to be a more discoverable interface where every feature in the product is easy to find and use. And the CEIP data was used to lay out the ribbon, placing the most popular commands where they can be most easily found and used. CEIP data was also used to find out what desirable features—features that users asked for—were rarely used, indicating that they were too hard to find.

One key indicator that Office needed a new UI was that four of the top ten requested features received from Word 2003 users were for features that were already in the product. People just didn't know how to find them! According to Jensen Harris, Group Program Manager for the Microsoft Office User Experience Team (he's the lead dog on the team that designed the new UI), features like adding a watermark to Word documents were so hard to find that a lot of users asked how to do it or didn't realize they already could. With Office 2007, the feature is prominently located on the "Page Layout" tab, and Jensen has had a lot of users comment on what a "great new feature" that is.

And Now, by Popular Demand. . .

Seeing as how you're reading a book on Outlook 2007, you've probably already bought it, so I'm not going to try to sell you on why you should go get it. Let me just briefly highlight some of the key new features of Outlook 2007 that lawyers are going to love. I'll explain them in more detail later in the book, but here's the teaser:

1. The To-Do Bar—A great new tool to help you manage tasks, appointments, deadlines, and action items (page 8).
2. Integrated RSS Aggregator—Subscribe to blogs and newsfeeds with Outlook, and get those items right alongside your mail if you use search folders (the RSS Aggregator is detailed on page 61, the search folders on page 38).

3. A new editor for creating e-mails—All the power of Microsoft Word, even if you don't have Word installed.
4. Instant Search—Helps you find items nearly instantly, even across multiple folders or multiple stores (page 38).
5. Attachment Previewing—Quickly read those Word documents from opposing counsel right there in the Outlook Reading Pane without having to open Word.
6. New views in the calendar—Improved views and color-coding make the calendar easier and more productive to use (Chapter 4).
7. Easy categorizing and flagging of messages for follow-up.
8. Calendar sharing and group calendars.

There are a lot more new features, like improved security and anti-phishing capabilities, postmarks, Free/Busy information management, and a lot of other subtle things that will really excite your consultant or IT person but might be a tad esoteric for you. I'll mention them throughout the book, but mostly I want to focus on the features and tools that you're really going to use and care about in your daily practice.

So, let's get right into it. Turn the page to Chapter 1, "A Tour of Outlook."

A Tour of Outlook   1

Let's start off by taking a tour of Microsoft Outlook. For those of you who are veterans of Outlook and are satisfied discovering the new nuances of Outlook 2007 on your own, you may want to skip to Chapter 2. For the rest of you, make some popcorn and let's take a tour.

The Explorer Window

A lot of folks don't realize that the main Outlook window—the one where you can work with mail items, calendar items, tasks, and other folders—is called the "Explorer." The Explorer in Outlook 2007 looks a lot like the one in Outlook 2003, which was the first significant Explorer design change since Outlook 97.

Let's start at the top. The very first thing you'll see is the title bar (Figure 1.1), which shows the Outlook icon, the name of the currently selected folder, and the product name. There is nothing terribly remarkable about the title bar aside from the familiar window controls on the right-hand end that let you minimize, window, or close the Outlook Explorer.

The title bar does serve one other purpose. When you have the Explorer windowed (sized smaller than full screen), you grab the title bar with your mouse to drag and drop the window somewhere else on the screen or to move it onto your other monitor if you're using a dual-monitor setup.

Immediately beneath the title bar you will usually find the menu bar. I say "usually" because it is possible to move and rearrange the menu and toolbars, and I find that a number of users have done so (almost always by accident).

Inbox - Microsoft Outlook

FIGURE 1.1

Lawyers and Dual Monitors

I have set up dual-monitor set-ups for a number of lawyers (and even a three-monitor setup for one), including several lawyers who grumbled that it was a waste of time and money. After a week of use, I have never had a single lawyer who was willing to let me take the second monitor away. The productivity gains and just general enjoyment of working in a dual-monitor setup are really quite impressive. Try it, you'll like it.

To move the menu bar, or any of the toolbars, just grab the little dotted vertical line at the far left end of the bar with your mouse cursor and drag and drop it wherever you like. In addition to reordering the bars vertically, you'll find that you can also "break off" the bars and have them float anywhere on the screen you like, or you can "re-dock" the bars to the sides or bottom of the screen if you prefer to have them there. Most users prefer to leave them right where they are, but the choice is yours.

If you have a bar "floating" somewhere else on the screen and would like to quickly return it to the top of the screen, you can drag it there or just double-click the title bar of the floating bar.

The menu bar contains the familiar "File, Edit, View" menus that you use to access features like printing, changing the current view, and so forth (Figure 1.2). At the right-hand end of the menu bar is the Help Query Field where you can type a question in plain language, and the help system will attempt to give you an answer. The help system has improved somewhat with Outlook 2007.

File Edit View Go Tools Actions Help Account Settings...   Type a question for help

FIGURE 1.2

The menu bar you see in Figure 1.2 is from one of my personal machines, and the sharp-eyed among you may have discerned that it contains a menu item that few, if any, of you, will see on your own machines: "Account Settings." If you're wondering how I did that, stick around. I'll tell you in Chapter 13.

Back to the Future

If you click any of the menu items you'll notice something has changed from the menus of Office 2003: The adaptive menus are gone. In Office 2003, clicking on a menu would bring down only a partial menu initially. Office would hide any commands you hadn't used recently and only display them if you paused for several seconds or clicked the double-chevrons at the bottom of the menu. This was intended to make the interface simpler, and it was thought that users would love it. It didn't and they didn't. So the adaptive menus are gone with Office 2007.

Beneath (usually) the menu bar, you will find the toolbar(s). Also a holdover from previous versions of Office, it is a little prettier and adds some buttons for new or improved features, but otherwise it's unchanged. Office 2007 has three default toolbars to choose from: Standard, Advanced, and Web. Contained on the toolbar is an assortment of useful commands like "New" (to create a new item), "Reply," "Send/Receive," and so forth. You can activate any of those things from the menus on the menu bar as well, but it's just a little faster and easier for most people to do those from the toolbar rather than having to dig into a menu. You can turn the toolbars on or off from the View | Toolbars menu.

Guess Who Else Is Gone?

"Clippy" the Office Assistant, whose popularity rating was only slightly better than Jar Jar Binks, has been retired. The new help system does not include an Office Assistant. If you really want a small dog to wag its tail and earnestly watch you work, I would recommend a Maltese.

Where the Action Is

Below the toolbars is the main part of the Outlook Explorer window, where all the work gets done. This area of the screen changes a bit depending upon which section (Mail, Calendar, Contacts, etc.) you have open at the time, so we'll start by looking at the Mail section.

Mail

The Mail section is where you go to deal with messages—both sent and received. In Office 2007 this area of the screen is generally split into four sections:

The Navigation Pane

The Navigation Pane is where you move through the various sections and folders of Outlook (Figure 1.3).

At the top is the Favorite Folders section where you can readily add the folders that you use most often. If you are a big user of search folders and subfolders, as you probably

Fun Fact

During the development of Office 2003, where the Navigation Pane debuted, it was known internally at Microsoft as "The Wunderbar."

FIGURE 1.3

To make the most of your Navigation Pane, figure out which sections you're going to use frequently and then use your mouse to grab the separator bar at the top of the section group list, and then drag it down until only those groups show as the full-sized groups. On my Navigation Pane in Figure 1.3, you can see that I dragged it down until everything below "Tasks" was shown in small icon format.

should be, then the Favorite Folders section is especially handy. Essentially, it gives you one-click access to the folders you use most often without having to scroll and drill through the often considerably more extensive folder list beneath it. You can add as many folders to the Favorite Folders list as you like, although obviously there are some practical limits that you will encounter. I generally find that it's best to keep your Favorites list to twelve or fewer if you can; otherwise the list grows so long that it becomes unwieldy. To add a folder to the Favorite Folders list, just right-click it on the Folders List and choose "Add to Favorite Folders" from the context menu that appears.

To remove a folder from the Favorite Folders list, right-click it and choose "Remove from Favorite Folders" on the context menu.

Beneath the Favorite Folders list is the Mail Folders list, which, as the name implies, is a list of all of your mail folders. This is a bit of an improvement over older versions of the Folder List that you might recall from Office 2000 in which all Outlook folders were crowded together on a single list. In Outlook 2007 (and 2003, actually) the Mail Folders list displays only the mail folders.

For those of you who actually long for the old Folder List, don't touch that dial. In a page or three I'll show you how you can still get that too.

The plus sign next to a folder name on the list indicates that there are subfolders of that folder. In Figure 1.3 you can see that I have a folder for "Clients" that contains subfolders for each of the clients my firm serves. You can create as many subfolders and layers of folders as you like; I encourage you to create separate matter folders for particularly active clients. In fact, not only do I encourage you to do that, but later I will show you how to process and organize e-mail by creating subfolders and sub-subfolders.

The numbers you see next to the folder name generally indicate the number of unread items within that folder. I say "generally" because you can configure Outlook to show you the total items in that spot instead. I'll tell you how in Chapter 13.

Continuing down the Navigation Pane, you'll find the section groups that let you change to the Calendar, Contacts, Tasks, or other sections of Outlook. By clicking on any one of these groups, the Outlook Explorer will change to show you that section of Outlook.

If you would like to reorder the section groups—for instance, if you really love the Journal and want that at the top of the list, or if you have an odd compulsion to alphabetize the list—you can click the little down arrow in the bottom right corner of the Navigation Pane and select "Navigation Pane Options." From there you can turn the display of various section groups on or off, or you can move them up or down in the list.

Out of Sight, If You Don't Mind

One piece of common feedback from Outlook 2003 was that the Navigation Pane sometimes took up too much space. Users would often spend a lot of time in a single folder—Inbox for example—and yearned to be able to dispose of the Navigation Pane, at least temporarily, in order to gain more screen real estate. With Outlook 2007, the Navigation Pane, as well as the folder lists, are collapsible so that they "fold up" out of the way. To collapse the Favorite Folders section, for example, just click the double-chevron icon along the right-hand side of it. That will cause the Favorite Folders section to collapse "flat" so that you can display more folders in the Mail Folders section. The Mail Folders section is collapsible too, although there doesn't seem to be any advantage to that.

If you'd like to collapse the entire Navigation Pane, just click the sideways-chevrons at the top right-hand corner of the Navigation Pane, and the entire Navigation Pane will slide away to the left side of the screen. Helpfully, it retains quite a bit of utility by allowing you to click the first few folders listed on the Favorite Folders list or one of the section groups below without having to re-expand the Navigation Pane. To re-expand it, click the sideways-chevrons at the top of the bar.

The Message List

The message list shows you the list of message items contained in the currently displayed folder. This is just like the message list that you had in Outlook 2003 with one notable exception: At the top of the message list is a powerful search tool. We'll discuss that search tool in considerable detail beginning on page 38, but its basic usage is quite straightforward: Click the field and start to type the term or phrase you wish to search for in the current folder. You will quickly see the power of Office 2007's new "Instant Search" capability. In fact, if you type slowly, you'll see the type-ahead search capability that starts to show you search results before you even finish typing and then narrows down the results as you add more characters to the query.

Beneath the search box you'll find the message list headers. Far from being merely dumb labels, these are useful little tools in their own right. Click the "Arranged By" header and you'll see a quick menu of a dozen or so different fields by which you can arrange the message list. Date is generally the default (Figure 1.4), but you will probably find Conversation, From, Categories, and even E-mail Account (for those of you who receive multiple accounts in your Outlook profiles) to be particularly useful.

FIGURE 1.4

We'll talk a little more about processing, sorting, and grouping your mail in Chapter 2, so get friendly with the message list—you're going to spend a lot of time there.

Reading Pane

The Reading Pane is an underappreciated tool for making you more efficient. In the old days you had to actually open an e-mail message in order to read it. An early Outlook innovation was the "AutoPreview" that would show you the first two lines of content of the message. That was a nice teaser and was occasionally enough to let you glean the substance of the message but usually still required you to open the message in order to read it. Not surprisingly, third party add-ins came out to add reading pane functionality to Outlook. Well, never a company to let a good idea pass it by, Microsoft added the integrated reading pane to Outlook 2000.

With Outlook 2007 you can choose to locate the reading pane on the right (my personal favorite), on the bottom, or turn it off completely. To change its location, go to View | Reading Pane. If you just want to turn it on or off quickly (to gain more screen real estate for the message list, for instance), there is a button on the toolbar that will do just that.

There are a few options you can control for the reading pane. Under Tools | Options | Other, you can find the Reading Pane tool (see Figure 1.5). There you can tell Outlook how you want the reading pane to treat your messages. You can have it automatically mark items as read after a few seconds of viewing or when the selection changes (when you change to another message). The last option is actually rather interesting and may require a bit of explanation. "Single key reading using space bar" lets

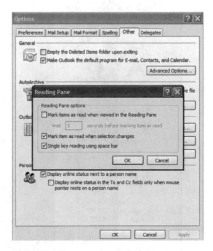

FIGURE 1.5

you use the space bar to scroll through the messages. When a message is selected, pressing the space bar will scroll through the message until it reaches the end of the message, then pressing the space bar again will take you to the next message. You can easily read through your entire list of messages just by repeatedly pressing the space bar.

The To-Do Bar

One of the new elements in Outlook 2007 is the To-Do Bar (Figure 1.6). The Outlook team invested a lot of effort around time and task management, and one of the areas that's manifested is in the To-Do Bar. The Tasks folder is one of the areas of Outlook that has always been somewhat underutilized. One reason for the lack of enthu-

> Time is Nature's way of keeping everything from happening at once.
>
> —Woody Allen

siasm for it has probably been that the Tasks haven't been readily accessible. Typically, folks get to the Tasks using the TaskPad on the calendar, but since most folks spend the majority of their time in the Inbox, it's just not very convenient to have to switch to the calendar every time they need to see what's next to do. The To-Do Bar eliminates that problem by bringing the tasks (and more) right out front, into the Inbox view, where you can work with them more readily. Adding a task is easy: Click the "Type a new task" field, and type the name of your new task. Press enter and you've just added a task that's due today. If you

FIGURE 1.6

click a task, you can open it; if you've completed a task, just click the flag on the right-hand end to mark it complete.

By default the tasks will be grouped and sorted by date, with today's tasks at the top. Overdue tasks will appear in red, the rest in black.

The Tasks list in the To-Do Bar brings more than just tasks to the party; the Outlook team recognized that very often e-mail contains an action item, and you don't necessarily want to create a separate task item for it. With Outlook 2007 you can use the "For Follow-Up" flag. We're going to get into the details of using this tool on page 30, but for now the quick version of the story is that when you receive an e-mail that you want to follow-up on, you right-click the Follow-Up flag and select when you would like to follow-up on the item. Outlook will put the item on your To-Do Bar.

The To-Do Bar also contributes a month navigator, handy for quickly seeing whether the 17th is a Thursday or Friday, as well as your next couple of appointments for easy reminders of what you have coming up.

So that's the quick tour of the Mail module. We're going to talk in-depth about working with e-mail in Chapter 2. For now, though, let's click the "Calendar" button on the Navigation Pane to see how we can work with the calendar to keep our schedules straight.

Calendar

The calendar is one of the oldest and best understood tools in Outlook. It's all about keeping dates and appointments straight. For an attorney, time is of the essence—the law is all about timelines, deadlines, statutory dates, extensions, appointments, meetings, conferences, filings, and, let us not forget, for most attorneys it is still the measure by which we bill our clients. Obviously, keeping your calendar straight and true is of upmost importance for the effective practice of law. Not to mention the fact that missing a key deadline could get us disbarred—never a good way to start the week.

Navigation Pane

The Navigation Pane for the calendar looks a lot different from the one we saw in mail, as you can see in Figure 1.7. The top part shows you the traditional date navigator, which lets you select different dates and do all sorts of magical things (I'll show you the best of them in Chapter 4). Immediately below the date navigator, you'll find a curious little bar whose purpose is not immediately evident. It says, "All Calendar Items" and includes a drop-down arrow. Clicking the drop-down arrow shows you a list of all the

FIGURE 1.7

data stores (see sidebar on page 14) you have that contain calendar folders with checkboxes to select or deselect them. The purpose of this bar is to allow you to initiate a search across all of your calendars. Click the "All Calendar Items" part of the bar, and the calendar area will go blank (awaiting search results), and you can type a search term in the search box at the top.

Below the All Calendar Items bar is the calendar selector, which shows you the different calendars you can view and search. At the least, you'll see "Calendar," but you may also see any other calendars you've created, any public calendar folders you have, and any calendars for other users to which you've been given permission. With the checkboxes, you can select which calendars you want to view, and you can view multiple calendars side by side. The calendars are organized into groups. You can create as many new groups as you

> Don't get too crazy creating calendar groups; otherwise you could fill the pane with groups and leave no room for calendars.

need by simply right-clicking any group header and choosing "New Group." If you have a lot of calendars on your list, you might consider creating groups for different practice groups in your firm or for different physical offices.

Below the calendar groups you'll find the Current View Pane, which provides a handy selector to let you choose whichever view of your calendar (Day/Week/Month, By Category, etc.) you want right now.

Below the Current View Pane (if you have it) is another new element in Outlook 2007. It's a pane of handy links that relate to the calendar. Some of these links (like "How to Share Calendars") will open Help File content. Others (like "Send a Calendar via E-mail")

Don't see the Current View Pane? It's probably turned off. Go to View, Navigation Pane, and check the "Current View Pane" item at the bottom of the list.

will actually launch actions. We'll talk more about these actions and links starting on page 98, but I don't want you to overlook this very handy new element of the calendar.

Finally, the Calendar navigation pane has the element that persists across all the different sections, and that is the bar that allows you to switch to one of the other sections (Mail, Tasks, etc.). The main work area of the calendar explorer is the calendar window. The view you see here will depend entirely upon which view you have selected. Yes, I know that seems obvious. The default view and the one that most folks use is called the Day/Week/Month View, and it looks just like Figure 1.8. We'll learn more about the details of working with the calendar in Chapter 4, but for now there are a few things I want to point out about this view. Let's start at the top. In Outlook 2007 you can change from Day to Week to Month views via the buttons at the top left. In Figure 1.8, I'm in week view, which is how I usually view the calendar because it's the most useful for me. The other important features you'll find at the top of this window are the radio

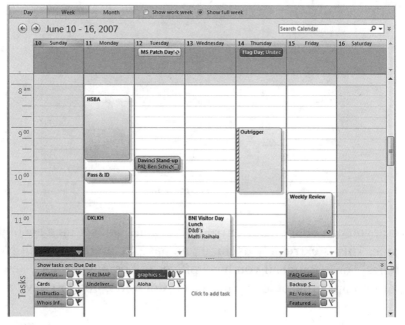

FIGURE 1.8

buttons that let you change from "Work Week" to "Full Week" views. (Naturally this only applies in Week view.) The key difference being that Work Week view only shows you those days which you have defined as your work week, typically Monday through Friday. On page 157 I'll show you how to change which days constitute your "work week" in case you're an associate and your work week is Monday through Saturday, or a partner whose work week is Tuesday through Thursday.

Just below the tabs that tweak the view, you'll find the date range displayed ("June 10–16, 2007" in Figure 1.8) and a handy pair of arrow buttons that you can use to move forwards or backwards in the calendar. On the right side of that same bar, you'll find a search field—search is very big in Outlook 2007—which you can quickly use to search across your entire calendar (or even to search your desktop!).

Down the left side of the calendar in Day and Week views, you can see the time scale. If you right-click anywhere on the time scale, you'll get a context menu that looks like Figure 1.9. Much of what is on this menu is actually only marginally useful. New Appointment, for example, is more easily invoked by just clicking the "New Appointment" icon on the left end of the toolbar. A few of the other options on this menu we'll talk about in more detail starting on page 91, but what I really want to point out here are the last seven options on the list. Clicking "Change Time Zone" will open the dialog box you see in Figure 1.10.

FIGURE 1.9

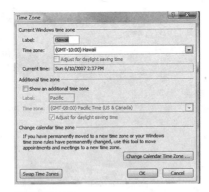

FIGURE 1.10

Here you can define your current time zone *and* set up a secondary time zone. This is extremely useful if you have to operate in multiple time zones. For instance, if you have offices in Los Angeles and New York, or perhaps your office is in Denver, Colorado, but you have a key client in Chicago, Illinois, by defining an additional time zone, you can have the time scale down the left side of the day or week calendar show both your time and the time in the additional time zone. This can save you a lot of mental math if you need to try and schedule a phone or video conference with somebody in that other time zone or if you just want to very quickly see what time it is there now. If you travel to that other time zone, a quick click of the "Swap Time Zones" button will change your primary time zone to the other one . . . and back again when you return.

The other element of the context menu from Figure 1.9 that I want to highlight is the time scale setting. You can see that currently I have mine set to "15 minutes," though the default is usually set to 30 minutes. If you're using Outlook to do very fine-level time tracking, you could set your time scale to be even finer—many lawyers bill in six-minute increments, and you can even view your calendar at that level if you like, but I find that view to be somewhat unwieldy. Play around with it; you can easily change the scale to something else if you decide you don't like it.

At the bottom of the calendar view, you'll see the new Tasks view. In past versions of Outlook, the task pane was set up alongside the calendar, and while that was useful, a lot of folks wanted to see their tasks listed on the calendar so they could see them right along with their appointments for the day. Unfortunately, what that led them to do was to abuse their calendar by adding tasks as calendar items. While there *is* a place for setting aside time on your calendar to accomplish tasks, I am hoping to discourage you from using the calendar in this way. The new tasks view, directly below the days on the calendar, will hopefully help with that.

One instance where putting the tasks on the calendar as appointments is sometimes handy is if you sync your Outlook Calendar to a PDA or phone and want to see the tasks and appointments together there. Still . . . I think it's better that the two remain in their respective places for most users.

To create a new task on any particular day, just click right below the last task on the list and type in the subject of your new task. How easy is that?!

There is one other view of the calendar that I want to highlight here, and that's the By Category view. If you're using your Outlook categories—and by the end of this book, I'll bet you are—you'll find this view a handy way to see all of the appointment items related to that category. It's also a nifty way to see, select, and copy or move all of the items on your calendar.

Contacts

The next folder I want to talk about is the Contacts folder. Contacts is one of the folder areas that is typically underused by attorneys, even though it is an extremely powerful feature. We'll talk more about Contacts in detail in Chapter 5, but for now let me just introduce you to it so that you'll be at least on speaking terms when we get there.

Navigation Pane

The navigation pane in the Contacts folder looks essentially the same as the navigation pane in the Calendar. At the top is the "All Contact Items" button, which gives you an easy way to search across all contacts in any information store you have access to.

An "Information Store" is a collection of information. Your exchange mailbox is an information store. An Archive.PST file on your C: drive is an information store. A public contacts folder is an information store. A SharePoint list is an information store.

Below that, you'll find groups of contacts folders that you have access to. By clicking on any one of them, you can view and work with that Contacts list.

Below that the navigation pane contains a Current View Pane that, just like in the Calendar, lets you change which view of the Contacts folder you have. There are several useful views of Contacts, and I'll point out a couple in just a moment here and give you more detail when we get to Chapter 5.

Below the Current View Pane you'll find a set of useful links similar to, though considerably more limited than, the ones you have on the Calendar folder.

So, let's get into the meat of the Contacts explorer. The default view of the Contacts folder is now the Business Card view that shows your contacts as a series of "Business Card" like objects in the folder. Figure 1.11 shows that view. This view is going to show you the key data on the contact: name, company, title, phone number, and address. Essentially, it contains the content you would expect to find on a business card. Between the search field at the top, the letter tabs along the side, and the ability to simply type ahead (just start typing, and you will be immediately taken to the records that match those letters), finding and using Contact items is extremely easy in Outlook 2007.

You do still have the familiar Address Card view (shown in Figure 1.12) also. This view displays much of the same information but shows it in a somewhat more space-efficient manner. For that reason, I personally tend to eschew the stylish business card view and opt instead for the classic Address Card view of my Contact items.

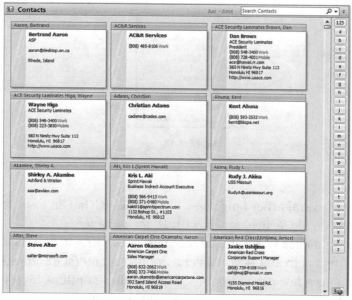

FIGURE 1.11

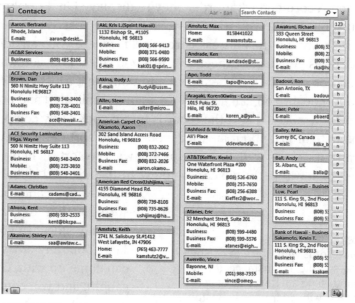

FIGURE 1.12

The sharp-eyed among you may have noticed a peculiar and inscrutable icon at the bottom right, below the alpha tabs. That button, which seems more in need of a screen tip than any button ever invented, allows you to add a second column of tabs to the alpha tab bar—a column based

FIGURE 1.13

upon one of several other languages like Greek or Thai. In case you have contacts whose file as field starts with Ω, for instance.

If you right-click the alpha tab column—with or without the Cyrillic second column activated—you'll get a context menu (see Figure 1.13), which contains a few useful options. Most of these options involve configuring the view. Let's take a look at the important ones:

- Show Fields—this lets you choose which fields are displayed for each record and what order they're displayed in. I rarely adjust this, but maybe you want to see a field like "Assistant's Name" or "Birthday" on the address card. This is where you can add them.
- Sort—as you might expect, this lets you select how you want the records sorted. Don't be fooled into thinking it's just A to Z or Z to A though. You can actually do some complicated and powerful sorts—you could sort the records by zip code or by company name or state or just about anything you want to sort them by. And you can sub-sort as well. So perhaps you want to sort them by zip code, but then within the zip codes you want them sorted alphabetically by first name and then sub-sorted within that chronologically oldest to youngest. Just about any crazy sort you can come up with, Outlook can do, and you can set that up right here.
- Filter—essentially the same as a search, filter will limit the items displayed to the ones that match criteria you specify.

> **Tip**
>
> Filter is the way to get a subset of your records with which to do something specific. For instance, if you want to send a letter to all of your contacts with addresses in Boston who are in the category of "Client," you could set a filter to match that criteria, and only those records will be displayed.

- Other Settings—lets you specify some miscellaneous view settings, the most important of which is probably "Allow In-Cell Editing," which is what lets you click on a field from right here in the

Explorer window and make edits to it without actually having to open the Contact item in an Inspector window.

- Best Fit—will adjust the size of your address cards or business cards so that they display in the Explorer window as efficiently as possible.
- Customize Current View—this is a quick and easy way to get into the tool that lets you change all of those settings plus a lot more in the design of the view. We'll talk more about customizing views in Chapter 12.

You might notice that the To-Do Bar is available to you right here in the Contacts folder. It's pervasive throughout the application so that no matter what you're doing, your time and task management is close at hand.

Tasks

The Tasks folder is one of the more underutilized folders in Outlook. We're going to try to correct that in Chapter 3, but for now let's get comfortable with the look and feel of it.

In Chapter 3 we're going to talk about how to create custom views for the Tasks folder to help you get things done more effectively.

Navigation Pane

The Navigation Pane in the Tasks folder follows the now familiar look of the Calendar and Contacts folders. At the top you have an "All Task Items" search link, followed by a list of the Task folders available to you.

 Turn on the Reading Pane in the Tasks folder—it'll save you having to open each item to work with it.

What's a little special about the Tasks folder's Navigation Pane is that the Current View Pane is particularly relevant here. The Tasks folder is one of the folders where you'll probably want to use various views depending upon how you're working with your tasks that day. Let's take a look at a couple of the different views that you may find useful:

Active Tasks—Shows you a list of task items that are not marked complete. The Simple and Detailed list views are fine but tend to get cluttered with completed tasks. The Active Tasks view filters out the completed tasks so you can see just the tasks you still need to do.

Next Seven Days—Shows tasks scheduled to be completed in the next seven days. Gives you a quick look at what's on the horizon for you.

Overdue Tasks—Lets you see the tasks for which you have missed the scheduled due date—great for catching up and self-flagellation.

Journal

The Journal is another one of those underutilized tools in Outlook. And especially for attorneys, whose job it is to track information and meetings, the Journal can be a very powerful tool. The Journal is all about tracking activities—I use it to track phone calls primarily—and, importantly, they include the ability to track the time spent on the activity. In Chapter 6 we'll look at how you can use the Journal to best advantage.

Navigation Pane

The Journal's Navigation Pane is very similar to the views we've looked at in the Contacts or Calendar folders. There are a couple of folder views for the Journal that are especially useful, however.

By Type View

This view shows a time line of your journal items, grouped by item type. It's an easy way to view your activities in chronological context (Figure 1.14). Note: You can view them . . . but counterintuitively you can't move them in this view, just open them.

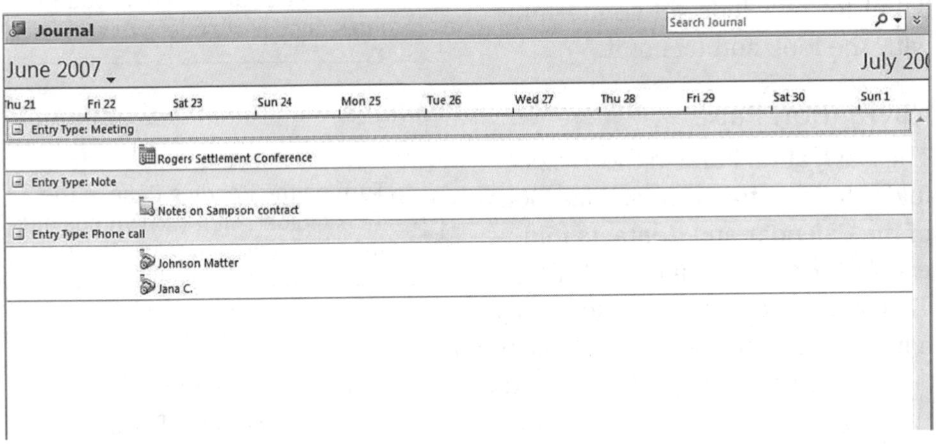

Journal									Search Journal		
June 2007 ▾											July 200
Thu 21	Fri 22	Sat 23	Sun 24	Mon 25	Tue 26	Wed 27	Thu 28	Fri 29	Sat 30	Sun 1	

Entry Type: Meeting
  Rogers Settlement Conference
Entry Type: Note
  Notes on Sampson contract
Entry Type: Phone call
  Johnson Matter
  Jana C.

FIGURE 1.14

By Contact View

The By Contact View, as the name implies, allows you to view your journal organized by the contact with whom entries are associated (Figure 1.15). If you don't associate a contact with your journal entry, it'll just list as "Contact: (None)."

There is another good reason to associate your Journal entries with the related contact, by the way . . . if you do so, the journal entries will

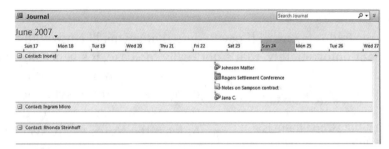

FIGURE 1.15

appear on the Activities tab of the Contact item. In Chapter 6 we'll talk about the Journal and how to associate an entry with a Contact item.

Last Seven Days View

This view as shown in Figure 1.16 is a table that shows you all of the recorded activities over the last week, sorted in date order (by default).

    This is an especially handy view for attorneys who don't capture their time in real-time so that you can quickly remember what activities you did in the past week—very handy for filling out or verifying those timesheets. Notice the "duration" field? I thought you might.

FIGURE 1.16

The Other Three

Outlook has three other groups that you'll find on the Outlook Bar. We won't spend a lot of time talking about them in this book, so I don't want to spend a lot of time on them here. They are sort of the linen closet of this open house—we'll open the door, look, nod, and close the door.

Folder List

The Folder List is arguably the most useful of the "others." Really it's just a window to see all of the folders and stores in your profile. If you're in the habit of switching folders frequently and don't want the features of the Navigation Pane, then the Folder List is a handy way to do that. There is also a useful folder that is only exposed on the folder list: Sync Issues. We'll talk more about the Sync Issues folder in Chapter 10.

Notes

The Notes folder is one of those folders that seems like it would be really useful, but unfortunately, that's not really the case. It's generally only useful to folks who have Windows Mobile devices and want to sync the notes they take on that device to their PC. At least the Notes easily synchronize using ActiveSync. And now with OneNote Mobile, even those folks will probably move to other solutions. The Notes folder is probably the weakest element of Outlook—the notes aren't

> **OneNote Mobile**
>
> With OneNote 2007 there is a mobile notetaking applet called OneNote Mobile. It lets you take notes, which will then sync using ActiveSync back to your PC and integrate nicely with OneNote.

sticky (i.e., you can't keep them on top of your desktop or move them anywhere). There isn't a good editor for the notes or even a reasonable amount of screen size. If you really want to type on a tiny yellow square, then I guess the Notes folder is your utopia. But I think Vista's notes gadget (Figure 1.17) is just as good and more widely available. If I was going to use Outlook for notes, I'd probably use the Journal to create them. I'll show you how in Chapter 6.

FIGURE 1.17

Shortcuts

The Shortcuts folder allows you to create shortcuts that point to other folders in Outlook. Can you create shortcuts to programs? Not easily. Can you create shortcuts to files? Not easily. Can you create shortcuts to Web sites? Wait for it. . . . not easily. That takes care of that.

Quick Access Toolbar (QAT)

In Outlook 2007's Inspector windows you don't have any way of easily customizing the toolbars as you do in the Explorer window and did in Outlook 2003. However, one small allowance was made for being able to customize a toolbar, of sorts, so that you can add frequently used commands to an easy location. That is called the "Quick Access Toolbar" (Figure 1.18), and you can add any command to it simply by right-clicking the button for it and choosing "Add to Quick Access Toolbar" as you can see in Figure 1.19.

FIGURE 1.18

FIGURE 1.19

You'll also notice that you can minimize the Ribbon from this very same menu—in case you want to reclaim that screen space.

Summary

The Outlook Explorer interface takes a little getting used to, but there is a lot of power in the views and searches (we'll really dig into search capabilities in the upcoming chapters). Understanding how to get around in Outlook is the first step toward more powerful usage of the product.

E-mail 2

Outlook, for most people, is all about e-mail, so I thought it best that we start our explorations right there. The chances are excellent that you receive a considerable volume of e-mail each day, and you're faced with having to decide what's valuable and what's not. Right along with that meeting invitation from your largest client or settlement offer from opposing counsel is a more dubious (or perhaps less dubious) offer for cheap male enhancement drugs or penny stocks.

Aside from separating the wheat from the chaff, or the SPAM from the ham if you will, effectively processing e-mail is about prioritizing, responding to, delegating, categorizing, and filing that e-mail in an efficient manner. This chapter will be all about the tools that Outlook gives you and some techniques that I'm going to teach you to do just that.

I'm also going to make an assertion that may put some of you ill at ease: you will be most effective and efficient when your Inbox has zero items in it! If you come along with me and accept my theory, by the end of this chapter you will have an empty Inbox, and you'll be enjoying the productivity benefits that result.

▼

I once assisted an attorney whose Outlook Inbox contained more than 18,000 e-mail messages in it. Sound familiar? Read on.

Why an Empty Inbox?

Let's start by looking at your Inbox. If you're a typical attorney, there are probably several hundred or even a few thousand e-mail messages in it. Check the status bar at the bottom left, and let's see where we're starting. Now, looking at your Inbox, you can probably see as many as twenty e-mail messages at a time. Without scrolling, tell me what the sixty-third e-mail message in your Inbox is about. If you can do it, I'll be truly impressed. Chances are excellent that you can't. Here's how that impacts you: Let's say you get a message relating to a case. It's from the client, and they're asking you to forward copies of some documents to them. You decide that you will be pleased to do so, but other items have a higher priority right now. You resolve to get to that request tomorrow. Between now and then you receive forty other e-mail messages, some of them important, some not. The message from your client asking for the documents has now scrolled off the first page of your Inbox. Did you write that request down anywhere? The typical lawyer doesn't.

Normally, attorneys don't bother to add minor requests like that to any kind of tickler or project management file. They feel that the task being asked for is minor and that they'll simply do it when they have the time. The problem is that out of sight is out of mind. The item has scrolled off your screen, and most people don't spend enough time scrolling up and down, especially if you have hundreds or thousands of messages in your Inbox. The item is at real risk of being forgotten, the client neglected. Have you ever scrolled down through your Inbox into the older messages and found a message from a few days or weeks ago that you never got around to dealing with because you simply forgot? It happens all the time. By keeping your Inbox trim and tight, even empty, you prevent this from happening. Outlook gives you the tools to file and deal with e-mail messages *and* not have to lose or overlook anything. You can be more effective and provide better service to your clients.

Arranging Your Messages: Sorting and Grouping

Dealing with thousands, hundreds, or even dozens of items can be a challenge if there isn't a rhyme or reason to the way the items are sorted and/or grouped. Typically we sort e-mail messages by the date received, and there are two pretty obvious ways to go about that: ascending or descending.

Ascending order means that the oldest e-mail messages are at the top, and as you scroll down the list you see newer and newer messages. As new messages are received, they are added to the bottom of the list. Not surprisingly this is referred to in Outlook 2007 as "Oldest on top."

Descending order means exactly the opposite—the newest messages will appear at the top, and as you scroll down the list the messages will get older and older. In Outlook 2007 parlance this is "Newest on top" (Figure 2.1).

FIGURE 2.1

So which is right and which is wrong? Neither is either. It's purely a matter of preference, and I'm going to suggest that even though you might prefer one for your daily work, there *are* times when you may want to switch to the other. Allow me to expand on this: Most people use the "Newest on top" sort for their daily work—I certainly do. But perhaps you're going to undergo a review and cleanup of your Inbox, and you have decided to start with the oldest messages first. If you're a Descending order person, then you're most comfortable working off the top of the list, so by reversing your sort to put the oldest items at the top, you can work through your Inbox from oldest to newest while being able to work in the format (top to bottom) with which you are most comfortable. When you're done with your review, one click puts your sort back to Newest on top—just the way you like it.

To change the arrangement of your Inbox, start with the "Arrange By" header, which probably says "Arranged By: Date." If you click on that header, you'll see other things by which you can arrange your folder. Some choices include "From," "Conversation," "Categories," and others.

I occasionally see users who sort their Inbox by "From"—in other words, by who sent you the message. This can be a very handy way to sort the Inbox when you're undertaking a big cleaning—trying to get from 1,500 messages to zero, for instance. You may well receive newsletters, sales fliers, or standard reports from the same user every day or on some other regular basis. By sorting the folder by "From" you can group all of those messages together. Maybe you don't need those twenty-nine weeks of "The Coffee Newsletter" that has collected in your Inbox. By sorting the Inbox by "From," you can group all of the messages from the same sender (e.g., newsletter@coffee.com) so that you can quickly file or delete them in one step. If you have subfolders created for each active case or matter, and every message from client@clientsdomain.com is relating to the *Client v. BadGuys* case, then by sorting by "From," you can take the thirty messages that client sent you and move them all to the *Client v. BadGuys* folder in one swoop. When I clean out my Inbox, I frequently start by sorting by "From" so that I can deal with big groups of messages like that all at once.

In a "By Subject" search, why do "Hi" and "RE: Hi" sort right next to each other? Because Outlook is smart enough to ignore everything before the first colon.

▼▼▼▼▼
Caution: Geek Material Ahead!
Conversation Versus Subject

One distinction not totally obvious to the user is the difference between arranging by Conversation versus arranging by Subject. If you arrange them that way, it probably looks like exactly the same thing, but there *is* a subtle difference. "Conversation" is actually a hidden field within the message item. When a message is first sent, the subject on the message is also copied to the Conversation field. The Conversation field is never changed again. If your client sends you a message that says "Let's Settle," then the Subject and Conversation are both "Let's Settle." And let's say you reply with a message attempting to persuade your client to stick it out and fight for a better result. Your reply, assuming you don't change anything, has the Subject as "RE: Let's Settle," and the Conversation is "Let's Settle."

Outlook is smart enough to ignore everything before the colon so the arrangement will still be the same whether it's by Subject or Conversation. But now your client has been persuaded by your professional advice and replies back to you. In replying the client decides to change the subject so that it now says, "RE: Let's Settle—Never Mind." When you receive that message, the Conversation is still "Let's Settle," but the Subject is "RE: Let's Settle—Never Mind." If you are arranging by Subject, this message will not be arranged along with the other messages in the thread; it will be arranged as a new thread all by itself. If you are arranging by Conversation, it will thread nicely right along with the previous messages. Outlook uses the Conversation field to keep all messages related to each other in the same conversation together, even if one or both users change the subject line.

▼

If you don't want your messages to group together, just sort, click the "Arranged By" header and uncheck "Show in Groups."

If you are categorizing your e-mail items (and if you're buying into my plan then you are), an arrangement "By Category" can be a very nice way to get all of the messages in the same category to group together. This can save you a lot of time by letting you work on all of them at once.

Processing Mail

So we want to get that Inbox cleaned out, and that means we need to start processing mail. This process cleans your Inbox and keeps it clean.

First of all we need to evaluate each e-mail message we've received, and ask some questions about it.

1. Is this message an action item? In other words, is there something here that requires activity? If so . . .
    a. Is this something I can do in thirty seconds or less? If so, do it. Do it *now*.
    b. Does it require something from *me,* or can I delegate this? If you can delegate it to somebody, then do. Click Forward, and send it along with any necessary instructions.
    c. If you can't delegate it and the message is going to take more than thirty seconds to deal with, your next question is: Do I have to do this now? How urgent is it? If it doesn't have to be dealt with now, then you should flag this message for follow up by right-clicking the follow-up flag icon as you can see in Figure 2.2. Select when you would like to deal with the message so that it is added to your To-Do Bar for that date. Once it's flagged for follow-up, move the item to the appropriate subfolder. (We'll talk about subfolders in just a few pages.)

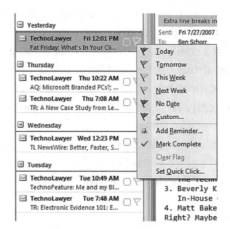

FIGURE 2.2

If this message is not an action item, or if you've acted on or delegated this message, move on to question 2.

2. Do I need to keep this message? You may need to keep this message if you need it for reference or if you want to schedule a follow-up to it. When I delegate an action item to one of my staff, I will usually save the original message in the client folder (keep reading, we'll get to that) and flag it for follow-up so that I can check back with the staffer after an appropriate period of time to make sure the item was properly dealt with.

If you don't need to keep this message, then get rid of it. Delete it. Delete it now.

3. Do I want or need this message? If it's junk, delete it. I am rather ruthless about deleting messages from my Inbox, *especially* if I've replied to the message or if it is part of a longer conversation. If I've replied to the message from Joe, then his original message is quoted in my reply, and if I ever need to go back and see what he said, I can just go to my Sent Items folder and pull up the reply to see what he said.

Subfolders

One of the more valuable tools in Outlook is the ability to create subfolders to organize your items. Subfolders, like paper file folders, can be created in any scheme that is comfortable for you. I generally recommend that attorneys create a folder called "Clients" and within that folder create a subfolder for each client. If necessary, you can create subfolders within the client folder for individual matters. General messages from or about a client can be saved in the Client folder; messages about a specific matter can go in the matter subfolder. In practice I rarely create matter or project subfolders. I find that I really only need to keep dozens or maybe a hundred or so messages about each client, and those are easy enough to work with in a single folder most of the time. Likewise, if the client has just a single matter, there really isn't a need to make separate subfolders under the client folder most of the time.

To create a subfolder, right-click the folder in which you wish to create the subfolder, and select "New Folder" from the context menu that appears. In the ensuing "Create New Folder" dialog box (Figure 2.3), give

▼▼▼▼▼
Beware of Rabbit Folders

Folders have a tendency to multiply like rabbits. If you're not careful you may find yourself with folders for each client, subfolders for each matter, sub-subfolders for each kind of communication . . . and then it just gets a little ridiculous. Keep it simple—unless you have hundreds of messages, it's best to keep them in one folder, and if you really have hundreds or thousands of messages, you should seriously consider if you really need to save all of them.

FIGURE 2.3

FIGURE 2.4

your new folder a name and, unless you need to change the folder type (i.e., the kind of items it will contain) or where it's located, click "OK" to create the subfolder.

That same dialog box seen in Figure 2.4, by the way, includes a couple of other tools for working with folders, notably the ability to Move, Delete, Copy, or Rename the folder. These are seemingly useful housekeeping tasks, though in practice I find that I use Rename or Move occasionally but Delete rarely and Copy almost never. That's because, while Rename is handy if I have misnamed a folder accidentally or if the name of the client or project has changed somehow, and Move is handy if I am archiving the folder to another storage location or if I want to reorganize my folders, I almost never Delete a folder (preferring instead to archive it), and I have no reason to create a copy of an existing folder.

Categories

Categories are another powerful tool to let you group messages together based upon the type of message. I use categories to delineate what group or classifications the item belongs to. My Categories include things like "Billable," "Expansion" (new business), "Personal," "Assigned to Danny," "Assigned to Jon," "To Review," "Speaking Engagement," "Writing," and so forth.

To use Categories just right-click the category square on the e-mail message to get a context menu similar to Figure 2.5. You can assign one or more categories to the message just by clicking them. The Quick Click option on the bottom of the list lets you select a default category that will be assigned if you just left-click the Category square on the message. I use "Billable" for my Quick Click category because that's the category I seem to assign most often—much to the delight of our CFO.

FIGURE 2.5

Flag for Follow-up

The Flag for Follow-up feature (Figure 2.6) is one of the most powerful features of Outlook when it comes to time and project management. It lets you assign a date by which you want to follow-up on the item, *and* any items flagged for follow-up will appear on the To-Do Bar where you can incorporate them into your daily project management process.

When you right-click the follow-up flag, you'll be presented with a number of options—some of them obvious ("Today")—and some of them not as obvious ("This Week"). Setting the follow-up flag to "This Week" will

FIGURE 2.6

give it a Due Date as the end of your current work week (which is Friday for most of us). Setting the flag to "Next Week" will give it a Due Date as the end of the next work week.

If you set the flag as "No Date," it will add it to your To-Do Bar but set it with no Due Date, which generally sorts to the top of the To-Do Bar. I used to use the "No Date" option for things that I wanted to do but didn't care when, but I stopped because I discovered two things:

1. Having all those items sorted under "No Date" was distracting for me visually. I like my "Today" items (which includes Overdue) to be listed first.
2. "No Date" was equating to "Don't Do." I found that I had so many items on my daily list to do that I rarely had time to address the items that were on the No Date list, and even though I didn't think those items were especially urgent the reality is that they were items that I did want to do at some point.

So now what I do is rather than assign "No Date" to those items, I assign a date somewhat into the future, often randomly. I click the "Custom" date option and tell it to set a date "+3 weeks" or "+2 months" or some such into the future. When that date comes along, these items will be there, and if I don't have time for them on that date, I can simply change the due date on the item and "snooze" it a few more weeks into the future. At least this way the item does enter my consciousness every few weeks or so and has at least a slight chance of being dealt with.

If the item is especially key, you should assign a reminder to it by clicking the "Add Reminder" option. This will open the dialog box you see in Figure 2.7, which is, incidentally, the same dialog box you get when you select the "Custom" date as the follow-up period, except it has the Reminder box checked and lets you specify the date and time you'd like a reminder to appear for this item. The speaker button to the right of the reminder time lets you select a sound file that you'd like to have played when the reminder fires.

You'll also see in Figure 2.6 that there are options in that dialog box for marking the item completed or for clearing the flag. It's actually easier

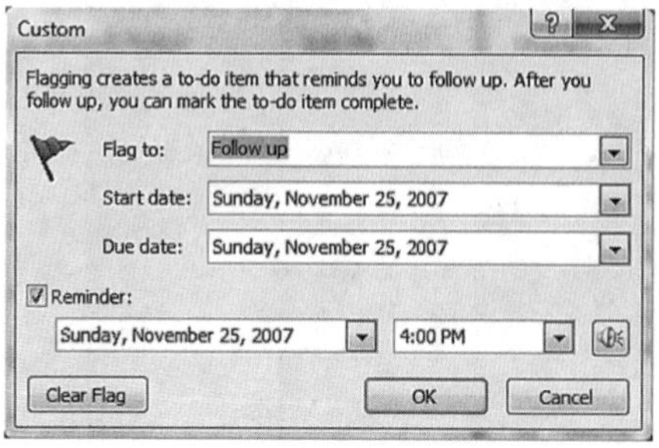

FIGURE 2.7

to mark the item complete by simply left-clicking the flag on the item again, which marks it complete. Clearing the flag, which you may want to do if you accidentally flagged an item, is most easily done by right-clicking the flag and choosing "Clear Flag" as you see in Figure 2.6.

The last option on the dialog box from Figure 2.6 is "Set Quick Click," which does the same thing that option does in the Categories dialog box—it lets you specify which of these options should be the default if you simply left-click the flag for the first time on a message. By default the Quick Click is "Today," but perhaps you'd rather the Quick Click be "Tomorrow."

Forwarding/Delegating

Forwarding a message to somebody is almost too easy in Outlook. With the message selected or open, just click the "Forward" button and type the address of the person or persons you wish to forward to in the To field. Note that any attachments will also be forwarded unless you explicitly delete them.

I often use the Forwarding feature to delegate something to a member of my team. If a client sends along a request I wish to delegate, I'll forward it to a team member, adding any instructions I wish to add. Then I flag the original message for follow-up, assign a reminder, and file it in a subfolder. When the reminder fires, I know to check back with the team member to see what the status is or, if I know the task was finished, check with the client to see if they were pleased with the results.

Creating Rules

Since Outlook 97, there has been a mechanism for automatically processing received mail based upon various criteria. In Outlook 2007, the Rules Wizard—which helps you create rules—can be found by going to Tools | Rules Wizard.

The Rules Wizard allows you to create rules that will be applied to messages automatically to do things like move messages into a subfolder based upon content or to whom the message was sent.

To create a new rule:

1. Click Tools | Rules Wizard to get the Rules and Alerts dialog box you see in Figure 2.8.

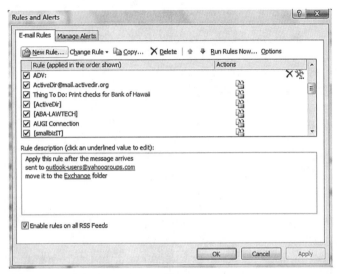

FIGURE 2.8

2. Click New Rule.
3. Choose the type of rule you want to start from. For the purposes of this exercise I'll start with a blank rule for checking messages when they arrive (see Figure 2.9). Click Next.

▼▼▼▼▼

It's in the Last Place You Look

A single message can be, under certain circumstances, acted upon by more than one rule. For instance, if you have a rule that assigns a category to a message and a rule that deletes a message, they might both fire if the message meets the criteria for both rules. Unless you specifically want a rule to only be part of what happens to a message, I recommend you also add the "Stop Processing More Rules" criteria to the message actions. This will not only prevent confusion among your rules but may, very slightly, improve performance as well.

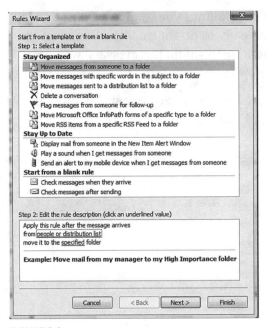

FIGURE 2.9

4. The Conditions dialog box will appear (Figure 2.10), which allows you to select what criteria you want the Rule to watch for. You can select multiple criteria, but keep in mind that these items are cumulative. In other words, it's "with specific words in the subject" *and* "sent only to me," not one *or* the other. Select the criteria you want.

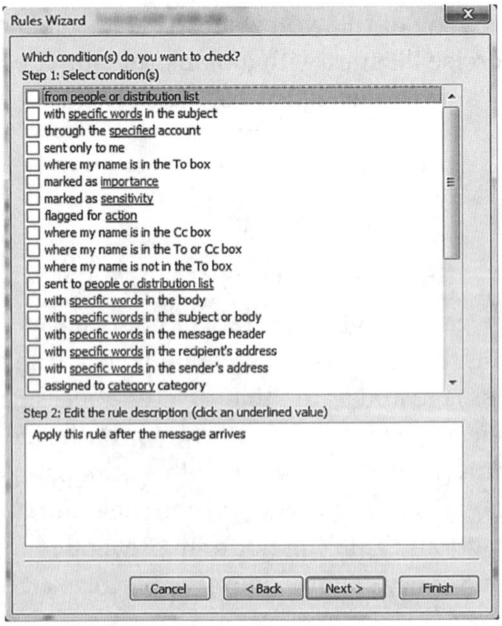

FIGURE 2.10

If you pick a criteria that requires you to specify a value such as "with specific words in the subject," click the underlined text in the "Edit the rule description" in order to open the dialog box to specify some text (Figure 2.11). Once you have specified the criteria you want the rule to look for and specified the text for that criteria, click Next.

FIGURE 2.11

5. The next dialog box (Figure 2.12) asks you what you want the rule to do with any messages it finds that match the criteria specified. You can have the rule move the message to a specified folder, delete the message, send a custom reply, or a number of other actions. Select the actions you want the rule to take, then click Next.
6. The Exceptions dialog box (Figure 2.13) will appear and give you the chance to specify if there are any exceptions where a message might meet the basic criteria of the rule but still not be a message you want the rule to fire on. For example: Perhaps you want all messages

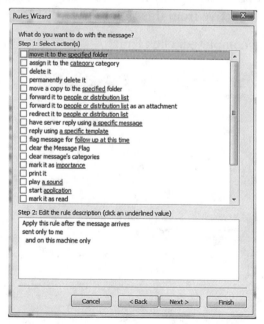

FIGURE 2.12

FIGURE 2.13

with a particular case name to be flagged for follow-up and moved automatically to a subfolder *except* if it was sent by your legal assistant. Once you've specified the exceptions, if any, click Next.

7. Now you've reached the last step of the Rules Wizard. In this step you'll give the rule a name that makes sense to you, and you have the option to run the rule now on the current folder (which is often a very good idea) and turn this rule on (or enable it) so that this rule will be active from this point forward (Figure 2.14).

With the rule completed, click Finish.

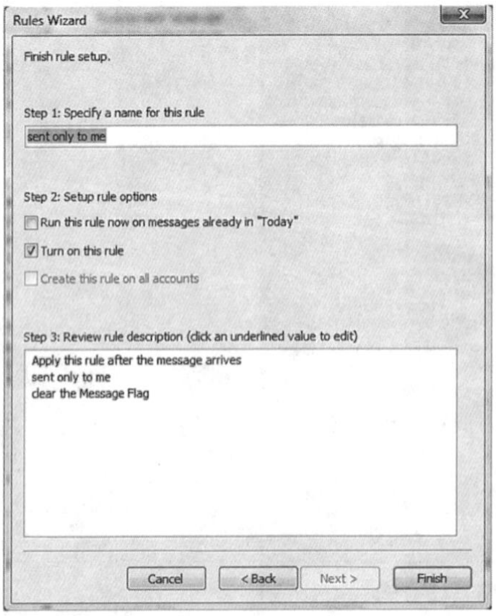

FIGURE 2.14

▼▼▼▼▼

Tricks of the Pros

The Rules Wizard can be a very handy tool for complicated mailbox cleanup. If you know a particular criteria that would identify messages in your mailbox that should be moved or deleted, you can use the Rules Wizard to create a rule that will identify and process those items then have that rule run now on the folder. You can even use it as an "as needed" cleaning agent by not enabling the rule to run automatically but merely to manually initiate it by clicking "Run Rule Now."

Client-Side Rules Versus Server-Side Rules

If you have an Exchange server, you'll discover that some of your rules are going to be client-side (which means they run in Outlook) and some are going to be server-side (which means they run in Exchange). The primary difference for you the user is that server-side rules will run even when Outlook isn't open while client-side rules will require you to be logged into Outlook. What determines whether a rule is client- or server-side is largely what that rule does. The guideline is whether or not the rule needs to access resources on the workstation (such as a local hard drive) or whether the rule needs to do something that requires the user to be authenticated (such as post to a public folder). If the rule is simply moving messages between folders in your mailbox, then it can run as a server-side rule.

Dealing with Attachments

Lawyers get a *lot* of attachments. Documents, exhibits, pictures, spreadsheets, scanned documents . . . can fill the mailbox in a hurry. Outlook is too often used as file storage for these items, and it really doesn't make for a very good document management system.

When you receive an e-mail message with an attachment, right-click the attachment and select "Save As" from the context menu shown in Figure 2.15 to save the document into your file system or document management system.

If there are multiple attachments and you'd like to save them all at once, select the message, click File | Save Attachments and you can then select to save all of the attachments to a folder at the same time (Figure 2.16).

<u>P</u>review
<u>O</u>pen
P<u>r</u>int
<u>S</u>ave As...
Remo<u>v</u>e
<u>C</u>opy
Select A<u>l</u>l

FIGURE 2.15

Practice Management Administrative Training Agenda_2 Day.doc
Desc of FO Admin Training and Scoping.doc
<u>A</u>ll Attachments...

FIGURE 2.16

Finding Your Mail

The first concern lawyers have with filing messages in subfolders is that they will have a hard time finding them again if they aren't located right there in the Inbox.

Instant Search

If you used a previous version of Outlook, then you are probably familiar with the experience of typing something in the search box, clicking Find, and then having the little magnifying glass icon go around and around and around for quite a while. Eventually, a list of messages that match your criteria may appear. With Outlook 2007, and in fact the whole Office 2007 suite, we now have "Instant Search," which uses the Windows Desktop Search (WDS) engine to constantly index your items (not only messages, but appointments, contact items, tasks, and more) in the background so that when you do a search, the search occurs against that index, and the results come back very quickly. You'll find a search window on almost every Outlook Explorer screen. Just type any key words or phrases you want in that window—the more specific you can be, the more precise the results will be—and press Enter.

Search Folders

Now that we're comfortable with the new Instant Search feature, let's talk about the next great tool for finding your messages in Outlook: Search Folders. A search folder is essentially a saved search. It's a virtual folder— it looks like a folder, but it's really just a view of a saved search. I actually spend most of my Outlook time in a custom search folder called "Today," which shows me all of the messages I've received today, across many subfolders. It's a handy way to aggregate received messages and make sure I see everything, even messages that the Rules Wizard has automatically filed into subfolders for me.

To create a new search folder, click File | New | Search Folder, or press CTRL+SHIFT+P. The New Search Folder wizard will start and give you

▼

Search folders actually debuted in Outlook 2003.

some standard options for your new Search Folder. The most common kinds of search folders will show you mail sent from certain people, mail flagged for follow-up, or mail in a particular category (Figure 2.17).

FIGURE 2.17

You can also create a custom search folder, which will display messages according to any criteria you like. If you choose to create a custom search folder (by scrolling to the bottom of the "Select a Search Folder" list and choosing "Create a custom Search folder"), you'll get a dialog box (Figure 2.18) that looks nearly exactly like the Advanced Search dialog box. In the "Search Folder Criteria" dialog box you can specify exactly how you want your Search Folder to behave.

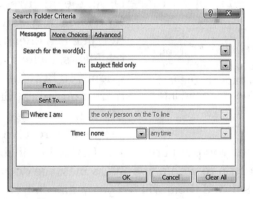

FIGURE 2.18

Creating a New Message

Initiating a new message is one of the easiest things you can do in Outlook. Click the "New" button at the left end of the toolbar, click CTRL+N, or click File | New | Mail Message. Once the message inspector opens, you need to address your message, add a subject line, type the body of your message, and send it. There's a reason why e-mail has become a popular form of communication—it's fast and easy.

Addressing the Message

Almost as important as what you put in the message is to whom you send the message. There are three fields in Outlook that determine to whom the message will go, and those are "To," "CC," and "BCC."

To

The To field means exactly what you think it means—to whom the message is being sent. You can put multiple addresses in this field, but be warned—everybody who receives the message will see all of the addresses you put in this field. If you're sending the message to a large number of people or to folks who don't want their e-mail addresses exposed to others, you should use a distribution list (which we'll cover in more detail in Chapter 5), or use the BCC feature that we'll discuss in just a minute.

CC: Courtesy Copy

You "CC" a message to somebody when they are not the primary recipient but you want them to receive a copy and you want the other recipients to know that they got a copy.

BCC: Blind Courtesy Copy

BCC is a special case. If you BCC a message to somebody, the fact that they have received a copy is hidden from the other recipients—hence the term *blind.* Any address you put on the BCC line is hidden from all of the other recipients, including other people to whom you BCC the message. In fact, there's no indication that you ever BCC'd the message to anybody. Those people who receive the BCC will see

> "CC" originally stood for "Carbon Copy," but since hardly anybody has used carbon paper in the last two decades, it has morphed into meaning "Courtesy Copy."

the recipients that you put in the To and CC fields of course. Word of warning—if a person to whom you BCC a message does a "Reply All," the fact that you BCC'd them will become immediately apparent since their reply will be sent not only to you but to all of the people that you addressed the message to and CC'd (but not anybody else you BCC'd).

Subject

The subject line of a message is deceptively important. A well-written subject line will get your message read and make your message more effective.

Here are some examples of poor subject lines:

- *Hi*
- *Important*
- *Do you want to get together for lunch on Tuesday, Wednesday, or Friday? I'm available all three days, and we could go to Art's.*

When you compose a subject line, it shouldn't be too brief and it shouldn't be too long. It's a headline. It should very briefly tell the reader what the message is about without trying to convey the entire message in the subject line.

Here are some examples of good subject lines:

- *Questions about Smith will reading*
- *Jones Deposition: Change of Strategy*
- *Let's make lunch plans for Thursday*

The only thing worse than using a poor subject line is using a blank subject line. Be sure to at least type something to give your recipient an idea of what the message is about. Some spam filters will actually block messages with blank subject lines.

Body

The body of the message is the meat of it—here's where your actual content is going. When typing the body of your message, try to stick to the rules of good writing:

1. Use paragraphs.
2. Use punctuation.
3. Don't type in ALL CAPS. It's hard to read and looks like you're shouting.
4. Try to write as clearly as possible.
5. Don't put anything in an e-mail you wouldn't put in writing.
6. Don't get overly cute with fonts. I once worked for a firm where one assistant liked to send her e-mail in a large pink script font. It was tiresome to try to read.
7. Don't get carried away with stationery. Outlook does allow you to create and use custom stationery, which adds graphics, colors, and backgrounds to your e-mail, but in most cases the stationery doesn't really add anything to the message and just makes the message unnecessarily large and difficult to read.

Signatures

The signature block is your sign-off to the message, much like a signature on a letter. A good signature block will include your name, your firm name, your e-mail address, phone number(s), and the URL of your firm Web site. You may also want to include your title and your postal address. You can edit your e-mail signatures from Tools | Options | Mail Format | Signatures, and you can have multiple signatures. Note that you can also specify which signature you want by default on new messages as well as on Replies and Forwards (Figure 2.19).

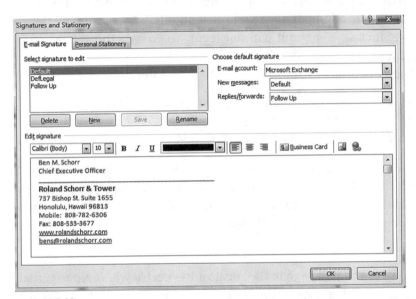

FIGURE 2.19

One way that law firms tend to use the Signature feature is to automatically include disclaimers at the foot of their messages. I'll leave it to you to decide how legally effective the disclaimers are—my own opinion is that they are probably not very effective at all—but I can tell you that excessively long disclaimers are quite annoying. If you really must put a disclaimer in your signature block, please try to keep it as brief and unobtrusive as possible.

Attachments

Sending attachments in Outlook is quite easy. Just click the "paper clip" icon in Outlook, and you'll get a dialog box that lets you find the file or files you want to attach. If you want to select multiple files from the same folder, you can hold down the CTRL key as you select each one.

Attachment Size

When you attach items, Outlook shows you in the list of attachments how large those attachments are (see Figure 2.20). Keep an eye on that—many systems and mailboxes have size restrictions. If you start adding a dozen

Attached: ☒ Can the Internet Really Provide Free Long Distance.ppt (1 MB);   ☐ factplace.txt (2 KB);   ☒ Office Deployment - Virtual Show.pptx (3 MB)

FIGURE 2.20

photographs to an e-mail message and each one is over a megabyte in size, you risk having your message rejected or filling up their mailbox or yours. If you have a few attachments and they are 50 or 60 KB each, that's probably not a big deal. If you have a lot of attachments and they are 1 MB or more each, that's a very big deal. Consider compressing the attachments (in Windows Explorer, right-click them and send them to a compressed folder, then attach the compressed folder instead of the individual items), or send the attachments in separate e-mail messages rather than all at once.

▼

Be careful about sending attachments to a large group of recipients. A couple of years ago, an attorney client of mine decided to forward a 2 MB file to his entire contacts list. More than 700 2 MB e-mail messages queued up in his Outbox, and clogged his firm's Internet connection for the rest of the day.

▼▼▼▼▼

Message Recall

Your biggest client has neglected to take your advice and has made a big mess of their case. In a fit of frustration you compose an angry rebuke and click "SEND." Moments later, when you've had time to breathe and take a sip of water, you think better of sending your client such a hostile message. "No problem," you think, "I'll just recall that message." Switching to Sent Items, you open the offending message, click "Other Actions" on the Ribbon (Figure 2.21) and confidently select "Recall This Message." The next morning you receive a reply from your client that says simply, "You're fired!" As many folks have discovered, to their dismay, message recall in Outlook quite often not only doesn't work but can actually exacerbate the problem. That's because there are various conditions under which not only will the message not be recalled but a second message, titled "Mike Sloan would like to recall his message" (Could you be any more stupid?!?!) will be added to their Inbox, instantly alerting them to the fact that you've said something that you regret. Here are some of the reasons for message recall failure:

FIGURE 2.21

- The offending message has already been read.
- The offending message has been moved to a subfolder, including by a rule.
- Outlook is not the recipient's e-mail client.
- Outlook is the recipient's e-mail client, but the recipient isn't currently logged in and has mail being forwarded to a Black-Berry or Treo. Or the recipient is checking e-mail via a Web mail client like Outlook Web Access.
- The recipient's mail server forces all incoming e-mail to plain text.
- It's a day ending in a "Y."

OK, so maybe I need to double-check that last one, but the other ones I'm quite sure about, and there are more. The reason for this dilemma lies in the way that Recall is implemented. Essentially, what happens is that when you select to "Recall" the message, Outlook generates a special message in Rich Text Format. That's the message the recipient often sees announcing that you would like to recall the previous message, and that's where things get dicey—those special recall messages are only processed by Outlook, and they're only processed if the message they are supposed to recall is still in the Inbox and is still unread. Of course Outlook has to be running at the time in order to process the recall message.

Bottom line: The old advice still holds true: Don't say anything in an e-mail message you wouldn't want your grandmother to read. Never click "Send" when you're angry! If you type something at all heated, save it to "Drafts," walk away, come back in a few minutes after you've had a chance to cool down, and re-read it before you send it. The "Recall This Message" function in Outlook often does more harm than good.

You might also consider posting the files you want to share with outside parties to some sort of secure file storage site that both you and they can access rather than e-mailing the attachments. Some of my lawyer clients who share a lot of files with clients have set up FTP (File Transfer Protocol) servers that their clients can log into in order to retrieve files or documents. The attorney e-mails the client a link to the files on the server rather than the files themselves. The client can simply click the link, log into the secured site, then download the files.

Encryption and Digital Signatures

For almost as long as e-mail has been around, computer security experts have warned that it is not entirely unlike a postcard in that it tends to travel around the Internet in a format that is relatively easy to intercept and read. To solve that problem, digital encryption solutions, like PGP (Pretty Good Privacy) were developed. Curiously, the legal community has never really embraced these technologies and still tends to send its e-mail unencrypted. Outlook 2007 supports S/MIME (Secure/Multipurpose Internet Mail Extensions) message encryption and digital signatures, which are quite secure and can be implemented fairly easily.

▼

Several years ago one law firm client of mine offered to encrypt all of their e-mail communications for their clients at no extra charge. Out of more than 100 clients, the number of clients who accepted the offer of free encryption: zero.

The first aspect of S/MIME is the *digital signature.* The digital signature acts very much like an ink signature on a document—it exists to provide authentication and non-repudiation—which are fancy ways of saying "to confirm that you signed it and to make it hard for you to deny you signed it."

The other element that the digital signature provides is verifying data integrity. Essentially, the digital signature includes data that can be used to confirm that the message received is exactly the message that was sent. This proves that the message was not altered or tampered with in any way in transit.

So the digital signature proves that the message was sent by the person it claims it was sent by and that the message received is the message that was sent.

The second aspect of S/MIME is *encryption.* A message that is only digitally signed is still sent in clear text, which means that anybody who receives it can read it. A message that is also encrypted appears only as gibberish to anybody who intercepts it. Only the intended recipient can decrypt the message and read the actual contents. S/MIME can't make the contents of the message any more intelligent, but at least it can prevent unauthorized folks from intercepting and reading it.

▼▼▼▼▼

Digital Rights Management

Microsoft's Digital Rights Management (DRM) is a fairly nifty idea. It lets you assign permissions to a piece of content: an e-mail message, document, spreadsheet, even a PowerPoint presentation. The permissions dictate what the recipient is allowed to do with that e-mail or file. For example, you can prohibit the other user from printing the file, or from forwarding the e-mail message. You can let them read the message but not edit it. You can expire the item so that in a certain amount of days the message or file just deletes itself and disappears in a very "Mission Impossible" sort of way (but without the smoke or inherent danger).

In a nutshell, the way it works is that it utilizes a DRM server that both parties can access. The receiving party has to authenticate against that DRM server before they can access the file or e-mail message. That is what enforces the restrictions or conditions. Now you might be thinking, "How can it possibly stop me from copying and pasting from the message? What stops me from using OneNote's Screen Capture function to just grab a bit of the screen and forward that?" Well, the DRM does. Screen clipping functions are disabled while an appropriately DRM-protected item is displayed on the screen. It's really quite clever. Of course, there's nothing you can do to stop somebody from pulling out their camera phone and taking a digital picture of the screen. There's nothing you can do to stop an authorized reader from calling their friend over and showing them the message on screen. But DRM does make it quite a bit more difficult for somebody to compromise or misuse your file or message.

Installing S/MIME takes a bit of work but isn't really difficult. First you need to obtain a certificate from somebody like Thawte or Verisign. There are both free and paid options for certificates depending upon your needs. Once the certificate is obtained, you import it into Outlook 2007 by going to Tools | Trust Center | E-mail Security, and click the Import/Export button right in the middle of the window—as seen in Figure 2.22.

That will produce the Import/Export Digital ID window you see in Figure 2.23, and you can browse to and import the certificate.

Once the certificate is imported, signing your mail is as simple as clicking the appropriate icon on the toolbar when you compose an e-mail

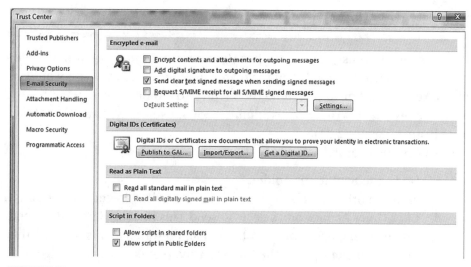

FIGURE 2.22

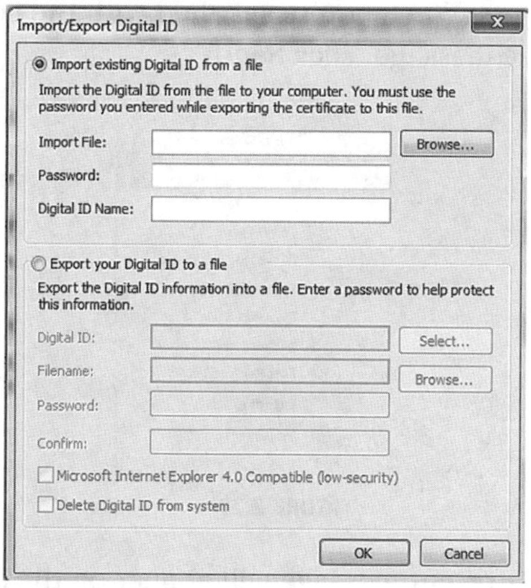

FIGURE 2.23

message. That will attach your public certificate to the outgoing message and confirm that the message is from you and that the contents are unaltered.

Encrypting a message is a little harder—you need to have the other party's public certificate first. The easiest way to do that is to have them send you a digitally signed message first so that you can then add them (and their certificate) to your Contacts folder. From that point you can encrypt any and all messages to that person simply by clicking the Encrypt icon on your new message inspector ribbon.

Resending a Message

Lawyers love to reuse content rather than rewrite from scratch that which has already been written. If you have an e-mail message that you would like to resend, either to the same recipient(s) or to new recipient(s), and either as originally written or with minor edits, use the Resend This Message feature (Figure 2.24).

To use this feature:

1. Go to the Sent Items Folder.
2. Find the original message on the list, and double-click it to open it.
3. Click Other Actions and select "Resend This Message" from the menu.
4. The message will reopen in the e-mail editor as it was sent. At this point, you can change the intended recipients of the message if you like, and/or you can alter the content of the message or its attachments. When you're satisfied with the content and recipients of the message, click Send.

FIGURE 2.24

Note that this resent message will appear on the Sent Items list as a new message, and the original sent message will not be altered in any way.

Reading and Replying

The other side of e-mail is receiving it. In fact, I daresay that you'll receive and reply to more e-mail than you originate—far more of my outgoing messages are replies than original messages.

The Reading Pane

One of the most useful and underappreciated features of Outlook is the Reading Pane. The reading pane allows you to read the entire text of the message without having to open the message. This is a major time-saver and is so effective that, in fact, I rarely actually open e-mail messages anymore. I just read them in the reading pane, and if they need a reply, I'll click Reply right from there (Figure 2.25).

You can locate the reading pane on the right side of your message list, as I have in Figure 2.25, or beneath it, as in Figure 2.26. Whichever way you prefer (I happen to prefer the right side), you'll find that the Reading Pane is a fully functional way to review your mail.

If you don't like the reading pane, you can also turn it off. The controls for right, bottom, or off can be found under the View | Reading Pane menu on the menu bar.

One of the other exciting features of the Outlook 2007 reading pane is the ability to preview Word, Excel, PowerPoint, and PDF files without actually opening any of those applications. Just by clicking on the attachment in the reading pane, Outlook will try to open the document in the reading pane so you can read it. First you'll get a security prompt asking you if you're really sure you want to preview the document. These

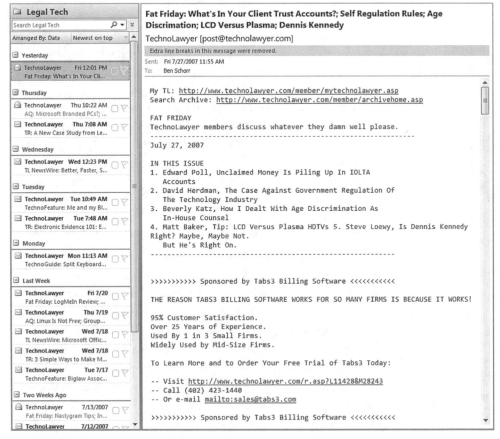

FIGURE 2.25

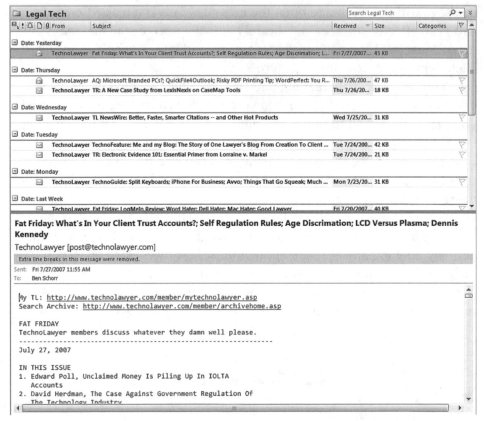

FIGURE 2.26

prompts sometimes generate complaints from users as overly heavy-handed, but unfortunately, Microsoft has been backed into having to put them in because otherwise they get blamed when foolish users open Trojans and other malware.

AutoPreview

AutoPreview is a concept that dates back for years in Outlook (Figure 2.27). It shows the first sentence or two of the message in the message list, so you can get a feel for what the message might be about before you open it. This can be handy, though in the age of the reading pane (as just described), AutoPreview seems just a bit anemic. Additionally, it is rendered useless if the person sending the message doesn't say anything useful or interesting in the first sentence or two. The other downside is that by turning on AutoPreview you reduce the number of messages that can be displayed on a single screen by approximately half.

To turn on AutoPreview just click View | AutoPreview.

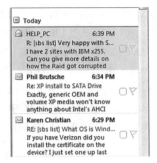

FIGURE 2.27

Quoting

When you reply to an e-mail message, you will generally include the text of what the other party sent to you in your reply—this is referred to as *quoting*. There are three major styles of quoting, and each has its adherents. Which you choose to use should depend upon the circumstances, and this decision requires a lot of personal judgment.

1. Top Posting. This is the most common kind of quoting—your reply appears at the top of your message, and the sender's original text appears beneath yours. This is good if the original message is fairly long, and your reply is less than a screen full. If it makes sense that your correspondent will just want to read the couple of paragraphs of your response without having to reread his or her original post, then top posting is fine.

2. Bottom Posting. In bottom posting, the original text appears first in its entirety, followed by your reply. If the original message isn't very long, or if you think the sender will want to reread what he or she said before getting to your response, this can be an effective way to quote. The downside to it is that if the original message was one or more screens long, it will require your correspondent to scroll down in order to see your response at all. I wouldn't use bottom posting to reply to a message longer than a paragraph or so.

3. Inline. Inline quoting is the trickiest way and is really only best used when the other person has asked several questions or made several points that you wish to address one by one. In this form of quoting you actually insert your responses into the middle of their post like this:

   - *How much do you want to offer as a settlement?*
   - I think we should offer $250,000.
   - *How long do you want to give them to respond?*
   - Let's allow them five business days to get us a written response.

Inline quoting can be a very useful way to communicate, but it requires some experience to get it right. One of the big dangers is that your text and their text will get confused, so it's important to use formatting to make it clear what they said versus what you said. Often the most effective way to do that is with the use of color—their text in black and yours in dark red, for instance. Inline quoting is not for amateurs, though, so practice with it before you try and use it in business mail.

Editing

It is sometimes useful to edit out extraneous text when you reply, especially if you're replying to only a portion of their e-mail. There are few things less efficient than a five page long e-mail with a single line reply. Edit judiciously, don't change meaning or context, but it's OK to trim down what you've quoted in order to save space and make your response easier to read. Their original text remains, in its entirety, in their Sent Items folder and in your mailbox where you've filed their message to you.

One other thing to note with replies—any items attached to the received message are NOT sent back when you reply, unless you reattach them. If you forward the message, however, the attachments are included.

Dealing with Spam and Viruses

E-mail is a critical business tool, but unfortunately, it is under attack. It's under attack by forces that seek to benefit or profit by flooding your mailbox with their own content or malware. Imagine if anybody could insert TV commercials into your programs whenever they wanted to. Every fifteen seconds your show is interrupted by a TV commercial, and even some of the commercials are rudely preempted by a competing commercial. Fairly quickly, you would just turn off the TV because the channel would just be a noise of jumbled messages. If you don't take steps to filter it, e-mail can be just that chaotic.

> **How Bad Is Spam Really?**
>
> Some vendors estimate that nearly 90 percent of all e-mail messages on the net are actually spam. I have an e-mail account with one of the free Web services that I only use when I buy something online, and it insists on an e-mail account— that e-mail account receives a spam message approximately every twenty minutes.

Outlook Junk E-mail Filter

Outlook 2003 was the first version of Outlook that shipped with a useful built-in spam filter. The spam filter works on a couple of different levels:

▼▼▼▼▼
Did You Know?

Junk e-mail is called "Spam" because of a Monty Python skit. In the skit, a customer has sat down in a café where nearly every item on the menu includes Hormel's SPAM lunch meat. The server reads the specials, and other patrons in the café start to loudly chant a song repeating "SPAM, SPAM, SPAM, SPAM. . . ," which effectively drowns out all other conversation in the café. In the early days of Bulletin Boards and chat rooms some abusive users would post the word "SPAM" over and over again, effectively shouting down other users, making conversation impossible. Thus the practice of flooding a communication channel with nonsense (or advertisements, which is often the same thing) became known as "Spamming."

a content filter that looks for words and patterns in the message that would indicate that it is likely to be spam and a blocked senders list that lets you define a list of people you don't want to receive e-mail from. The content filter works fairly well, and you can configure its basic sensitivity (see Chapter 9 for more detail on this) to be high or low. The blocked senders list is nearly useless, however, as spammers spoof the addresses they're sending from anyhow; you could easily fill the blocked senders list and nary make a dent in the spam.

Third-Party Anti-Spam Tools

There are numerous third party anti-spam tools, and they fall into three basic categories: hosted, server-side, and client-side.

Server-Side

A server-side anti-spam service attempts to filter spam out of your e-mail before it ever reaches your Microsoft Outlook client. This may happen at your mail server or even before it. Microsoft's Exchange Server 2003 or later has several server-side anti-spam tools. This isn't the proper venue to detail how to use them. Your Exchange mail administrator should already know, but I'll mention them here and give you a basic idea of what they do.

- *Intelligent Message Filter (IMF):* This is the most sophisticated of Exchange's anti-spam tools. It looks at each message based upon format, content, and other characteristics and assigns the message an SCL (Spam Confidence Level) number between zero and nine. Zero means that the message is definitely not spam while nine means that the message is definitely spam. The IMF can then

I deployed the IMF for one client, and it immediately cut his daily spam count from nearly 200 to about 7.

be told to take action based upon a threshold of SCL. For example, any messages that score an eight or higher can be automatically deleted while any messages that score a five or higher can be automatically placed in the recipient's Junk E-mail Folder. Be careful about automatically deleting messages, as opposed to quarantining them, due to the possibility (however remote) that you may have some false positives (legitimate messages wrongfully convicted as spam) that get deleted. The IMF's signature file is frequently updated by Microsoft to reflect new trends in spam. For maximum effectiveness, you want to make sure that you are continually applying those updates. The updates can be applied manually, or if you use the Windows Software Update Services (WSUS), they can be applied automatically.

- *Connection Filter:* There are a number of online Realtime Black List (RBL) services that you can configure Exchange to use. The way these work, basically, is that when an e-mail message is received, the Exchange server will check the sending e-mail server against one or more of these RBL services. If that server is listed as a known (or suspected) spammer, the message can be discarded automatically. Spamcop and Spamhaus are two of the better known RBL providers.

- *Recipient Filter:* Here you can specify addresses that should not receive any e-mail from the outside. Generally speaking this isn't terribly effective, though there is a handy setting on this filter that lets you tell it to discard messages sent to addresses that aren't in your directory. In other words, if you receive a message intended for an e-mail address that doesn't exist in your organization, it will just discard it.

- *Sender Filter:* This lets you specify senders (or domains) from whom you don't wish to receive any e-mail. While a popular concept, this really isn't a terribly effective way to stop spam because spammers tend to spoof their From addresses and change them constantly. While you might want to go ahead and block "@cheap-drugs.com," the reality is that most spammers are going to send from bogus domain names, and it would require far too much administrative time to try and add them all to your Sender Filter. There is one useful setting in the Sender Filter, however, that lets you filter out messages with a blank sender. No legitimate messages should have a blank sender.

- *SenderID Filter:* This filter is an idea whose idea has not yet come. SenderID is the e-mail equivalent of Caller ID in that it promises to help identify who the sender of an e-mail *really* is. The SenderID filter in Exchange can be configured to block messages that do not have the proper SenderID information. At this point, however, only a small minority of e-mail servers are configured to use SenderID, so if you configure Exchange to block the ones who don't use it, you're going to block a *lot* of legitimate e-mail.

Other server-side anti-spam solutions exist as well. Some of them are appliances that you can install virtually in front of your e-mail server and that attempt to identify and block spam. In many cases your firm's firewall may have the capability to check for spam and perform some filtering. The appliances aren't inexpensive, so I generally recommend that you try the built-in features like IMF first and see if the results are acceptable. If the IMF and other built-in Exchange tools can cut your spam to an acceptable level for free, then it probably doesn't make much sense to buy an expensive appliance.

> At one client more than two-thirds of the messages received by their Exchange server are rejected by their connection filters. That amounts to thousands of spam messages per day.

Hosted

Hosted anti-spam solutions are services like Postini or Pau Spam, which review all of your e-mail and try to filter out spam and malware before it ever arrives at your server. These outside service providers are going to charge you a monthly fee for the service. You'll have to decide if you think it's worth it to spend the money for those solutions as opposed to using Exchange and/or Outlook's built-in anti-spam features.

Client-Side

Client-side anti-spam tools run on the workstation itself. Outlook has its own anti-spam filter as we've just discussed, but there are also third-party tools such as McAfee's Spamkiller or the open source "SpamBayes" product. These products typically rely upon signature files to search incoming mail for patterns or phrases that might identify it as spam and then they quarantine it.

Antivirus and Antispyware Software

A substantial percentage of the mail on the Internet that isn't spam is actually some kind of malware: virus, Trojan, spyware, or something similar. Some anti-spam tools will also filter out viruses and Trojans, but you should be sure that you're running a purpose-built anti-virus tool as well. Like anti-spam tools, there are both server-side and client-side antivirus programs, and the best practice is to run one of each.

A good antivirus program will run in the background and automatically scan every message received so that it can quarantine any that contain suspicious content.

Critical: Most antivirus software relies upon signature files to identify malware, and as there is new malware released every day, it is essential that your antivirus software be kept up to date. Make sure that it is updating automatically at least several times a week, if not every day. All reputable antivirus products (at least the ones that rely upon signature files) include a mechanism for automatically getting frequent updates across the Internet whenever you are connected.

Increasingly, antivirus software includes an antispyware module as well, or if you run Vista as your operating system, you probably already have Windows Defender as your antispyware tool.

Going Away?

Sooner or later all of us have to take some time off and get away from the office. E-mail doesn't take a vacation though, so how do you handle those messages that come in while you're off getting some much needed rest and relaxation (or attending that out-of-town conference)?

Blackberries, Treos, and Other Little Addictions

Technology has allowed us to take our mailbox on the road. Most of us have mobile phones or other devices capable of letting us do rudimentary e-mail from anywhere we can get a cell signal. The Blackberry was the first major device that made it easy to get your e-mail while you were sitting in a meeting across town, and it became so addictive that techies nicknamed them "Crackberries" (Figure 2.28).

FIGURE 2.28

These days, it's not at all uncommon to look around the conference table at a meeting and see one or more people with their hands under the table, heads down, intently scrutinizing their laps. Of course, we all know they're checking their e-mail.

Today the Treo (Figure 2.29) has become a viable competitor to the Blackberry; in fact, I carry a Treo myself and find it a great way to keep up on my e-mail when I'm away from the office.

Microsoft's Exchange Server 2003 with Service Pack 2 supports a technology called Exchange ActiveSync, which will allow you to push your mail to any mobile device (such as a Treo) that supports Exchange ActiveSync.

Configuring Exchange ActiveSync is as simple as running the setup wizard on the mobile device and providing it with the same settings you use to access Outlook Web Access: the Web URL and your username and password. Exchange ActiveSync can be configured to send your mail as it arrives or to send it on a schedule such as every ten minutes, every hour, and so forth. You can also set it up for different settings at different times of day. For instance, from 6:00 a.m. to 6:00 p.m. on Monday through Friday, it will send your mail as it arrives. The rest of the time it will send mail every hour, for example.

Not All Treos Are Created Equal

Though the Treo device is manufactured by Palm Computing, not all Treos run the Palm operating system. In fact, quite a few use the Windows Mobile operating system. While the Palm-based Treos can be configured to sync with Outlook, in my experience the Windows-based Treos are easier and more reliable to configure for Exchange ActiveSync.

Push Versus Pull

Push e-mail sends your mail to your device as it arrives, without requiring any action on your part. Pull e-mail requires you to affirmatively initiate the checking of the mail.

FIGURE 2.29

The Blackberry requires a redirector of some sort. The redirector is a piece of software that monitors your mailbox and "redirects" received messages to your Blackberry device. That redirector can be a piece of software that runs on your computer; it can run on a server, or some of the providers like Verizon have a service that runs on a Web site that does it. Keep in mind that the different solutions have different advantages and disadvantages: Some don't forward attachments, for instance, while the redirector that sits on your personal computer requires your personal computer to be left on and logged in to work. That said, the Blackberry is a mature, widely deployed, and well-understood technology that generally serves its users well.

Outlook Web Access

Since Exchange 5.0, Microsoft's Exchange Server has included a technology that is currently called "Outlook Web Access." The technology has evolved greatly over the years, becoming more usable and capable and more "Outlook-like." This book is not long enough for a comprehensive look at Outlook Web Access, but several resources exist with that information if you wish to learn more.

Outlook Web Access (OWA) allows you to use a Web browser from any Internet-connected computer to connect to your server and check your e-mail. It can be very useful from an airport Internet kiosk, a hotel business center, or your brother's home computer when you're visiting on vacation. In Exchange Server 2003, OWA has evolved to include many of the standard Outlook features including right-click context menus and the ability to access all of the folders in your mailbox (including subfolders).

Three Ways Your Assistant Can Review Your E-mail Without Compromising Your Pass Phrase

I can't tell you how many times I've been in a law firm and heard a lawyer say, "I'm leaving on vacation tomorrow. Here's my password, please log in and check my e-mail while I'm gone." While the intent is noble, it's a horrible idea. With your username and password, your assistant is effectively you. If he or she wants to send an e-mail while you're gone—like an e-mail to the managing partner suggesting a raise for him or herself—it's being sent as you. Additionally, when your assistant is logged in as you, they have access to everything you have access to. That can include time and billing data and potentially other sensitive firm data like financial or payroll information. Access to all of the other messages in your mailbox—including that "HR" folder you have containing e-mails detailing which members of the firm are about to get fired—is available. If you really need your assistant to check your mail while you're away, here are a few better ways to do it:

1. Have your mail automatically forwarded to your assistant's account temporarily. He'll see your mail in his Inbox and can deal with it if necessary but doesn't have access to the rest of your mailbox and can't access other firm systems as you. You can either have the messages redirected to him and he can save for you only those messages you'll need to see when you get back, or you can have copies of the messages sent to him—leaving the original in your mailbox so that you'll still see all messages when you get back.

> **Caution!**
>
> If your assistant is reviewing your mail while you're away, he's going to see everything. Be sure to warn your partners and other key firm personnel that your assistant is reading your mail so that they are careful about sending you any messages while you're away that they wouldn't want the assistant to see. You may want to extend that warning to your family and friends as well—it would be potentially embarrassing if your spouse sent you a spicy love message that ends up in your assistant's hands.

2. Give your assistant's account permissions to your Inbox while you're away, and let her open it from her own computer. This requires a bit more effort but doesn't require any forwarding to be set up. Be careful about giving permissions to subfolders as well—you probably don't want your assistant reading the messages from your mom in your "Personal" folder where she discusses Dad's colonoscopy in great detail.

3. If you must have your assistant log into your computer as you, change your pass phrase before you leave and give the assistant the changed pass phrase. When you return, change it back or to something new.

Why the Out-of-Office Message Is a Dubious Proposition

One of the popular requests in the Outlook newsgroups is for assistance with the Out-of-Office Assistant. This is a feature in Outlook that will automatically send a reply to people who e-mail you with a pre-created message that says something like

> *Thanks for your message. I'm on vacation until March 3. If this message is urgent, please call my assistant Chris at (808) 555-1212. Otherwise, I will be sure to get back to you as soon as I return.*

This seems like a good idea, but it has three notable shortcomings:

1. It potentially tells spammers who have been lucky enough to get their message through to your mailbox that they have stumbled upon a legitimate mailbox. This is a surefire way to get your

address sold to an army of other spammers and get a substantial amount of additional spam.

2. It tells potential criminals that you're away. How hard is it to find your home address given your name and place of employment?

3. You may not want to tell all of your clients or opposing counsel that you're away. Better to have your assistant notify just those clients who need to know.

Unified Messaging

The holy grail of computer messaging has long been "Unified Messaging" or "UM," which promises to bring all of our varied communications into a single location.

Faxes

Though the fax is going the way of the dinosaur, the only industry that seems to still cling to facsimile technology as much as the legal field is the medical field. How medical use of fax complies with HIPAA requirements is a subject for a different work, but how faxes are received and distributed is still a major cause of concern for lawyers. Sending and receiving faxes electronically is a more efficient solution than paper, and there are a number of fax solutions available that can integrate with Outlook. Some of those solutions come in the form of software that runs on a server and routes received faxes to your mailbox. Others are third-party services, like eFax, that receive your faxes and send them to you via e-mail.

Whichever solution you choose, the convenience of having your faxes delivered to your Inbox means never again having to pace back and forth to your secretary's Inbox to see if that important fax has come in yet. If you have a mobile device like a Blackberry or Treo as we discussed previously, then you can even find out if the fax has arrived (and in many cases read it) from wherever you are!

Voicemails

Voicemail is an essential communication medium in the legal field. All of you get voicemails every business day. Typically, you have to check your voicemails separately from your e-mail, but Unified Messaging aims to change that by putting your voicemails in your Inbox.

Most new phone systems support locating the voicemails in your Exchange Server mailbox, but the way they implement that can vary widely. Some will store the voicemails in the Exchange mailbox itself. Some will store the voicemails on a separate voicemail server, more like traditional voicemail systems operate. Some of those who store the message on the separate server will put a link to the voicemail message in your Exchange mailbox while others will require you to configure Outlook to see the Voicemail server as a separate message store so that you will have your traditional Inbox as you're accustomed to and a voicemail Inbox, which is a separate folder.

If you have a Blackberry or Treo that supports the playing of sound files, most of the unified messaging systems will allow you to play your messages through the device. The voicemail sound file simply appears as an attachment to the message, which you can click to play on the mobile device.

If your particular system doesn't support that method, then there is always the old-fashioned way of listening to the message: call your voicemail system from any phone, and have the system play back your message(s) to you.

RSS

RSS or "Really Simple Syndication" is a popular Web format used to publish frequently updated content such as news articles or blog entries. RSS feeds can be found on many different sites from news to sports to technology. They're extremely handy for keeping track of sites or subjects that you would normally have to check on manually. By subscribing to the RSS feed, any new content is sent to you automatically, and you don't have to remember to check that site. Accordingly, you get notified of new content on a much more timely basis. Today, almost any site with regularly updated articles or content may have an RSS Feed.

If you're using Internet Explorer 7 or Mozilla, the RSS Feed icon on the toolbar will light up if the browser detects an associated RSS Feed that you can subscribe to (Figure 2.30). Subscribing to a feed in Internet Explorer 7 will automatically add it to your RSS Feeds list in Outlook if you have Outlook configured to sync its RSS Feeds to the Common Feed List (Figure 2.31). When you first start Outlook, it will ask you if you'd like to sync its RSS feeds to the Common Feed list. If you want to change that setting later, you can do so on the Tools | Options | Other | Advanced Options dialog. If you would like to manually add an RSS feed to Outlook, follow these steps:

FIGURE 2.30   **FIGURE 2.31**

1. Go to the feed page and copy the URL (which looks like this: http://news.google.com/news?ned=us&topic=n&output=rss) from the address bar of your browser.

2. Go to Tools | Account Settings and click the RSS Feeds tab.
3. Click New.
4. Paste that URL into the New RSS Feed dialog box as you see in
    Figure 2.32.

FIGURE 2.32

After you click "Add," Outlook will pop up a summary page, which
seeks to confirm the default settings for the RSS feed. Click OK to accept
the defaults, and Outlook will add the new RSS feed to your list, create a
subfolder for it, and start to download content (Figure 2.33).

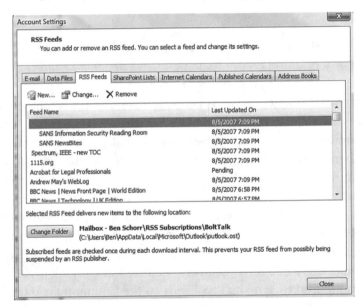

FIGURE 2.33

Summary

E-mail is the "killer application" for Outlook, and it's what the vast majority of users spend most of their Outlook time doing. Learning to handle
e-mail effectively is one of the best ways to become a more effective Outlook user and, as law and business becomes increasingly e-mail focused,
a more effective lawyer. Using flags, subfolders, and search folders you
can keep your Inbox lean and clean in order to be more effective in your
daily work. Outlook 2007 has enhanced e-mail by adding tools for processing large volumes of e-mail more effectively and bringing the increasingly
popular RSS Feeds right into the message store.

Handling To-Dos

3

A lot of work has been done in Outlook 2007 around task, time, and project management. In previous versions of Outlook, the Tasks folder has been one of the more underutilized features of the product. One reason for that lack of utilization was probably that accessing the tasks lists was not as convenient as it might have been. The user either had to go to the tasks folder, to Outlook Today, or, more likely, to the Task Pane on the calendar. With Outlook 2007 the tasks have been brought right out front with the new To-Do bar, which lets you work with your tasks right from the screen where you spend so much of your day—the Inbox.

To-Do Bar

The To-Do Bar is one of my favorite features of the new Outlook (Figure 3.1). It very cleverly contains not only your upcoming appointments and pending task items but *also* any e-mails that you've flagged for follow-up. This gives you one easily accessible place to see everything you need to do. Think about that for a moment—the sheer power of it. Used properly, it is a command center for your life and your practice.

Sorting

By default, items can be arranged by a number of criteria, by far the most common being Due Date. Click the "Arranged By" header to select from a set of other options.

FIGURE 3.1

▼▼▼▼▼

TIP: Priority Matters

If there is one weakness of the To-Do bar, it's that it doesn't give you any way to readily tell what the importance of an item is (high, normal, low). The way I do it is with automatic formatting. Right-click the "Arranged By Header," choose "Custom" and then click the "Automatic Formatting" button. Click "Add" to create a new rule, give it a name, then click the Font button to select a font it will display in—I opt for a slightly larger font size and boldfaced. You might also want to apply a color. Then click the "Condition" button, go to the "More Choices" tab and check the box that says "Whose Importance Is," and set the pick field to "High." Click OK all the way back out (make sure the checkbox in front of your new rule is checked so it will be active). Now any high importance items on your To-Do Bar will have the font attributes you just assigned in order to help them stand out more readily.

Due Date

Sorting by Due Date is the most common way to use the To-Do Bar, and it's no surprise since that is the default option. In all honesty, though, most of us are going to want to address our To-Do items in roughly chronological order—those items due first will be done first. Within the due date, you may want to sort by priority. Unfortunately, Outlook doesn't give us an easy way to create that sub-sort within the To-Do Bar, but in the box below I'll show you how to create a custom view that gives you that view.

Categories

The second sort that you may want to use is "By Category," which essentially groups items of the same category together. If you're using categories to identify which matter an item belongs to, to label items as "Law Practice Management" or "Marketing," then it can be handy to bring together all of the pending tasks in a particular area so that you can work on that area or matter more readily.

Importance

Perhaps you just want to see what your high priority items are first? Change your sort to "Importance," and the items flagged as high priority will be sorted to the top of the list regardless of their due date.

▼▼▼▼▼
Creating the Custom View

I prefer to sort my To-Do Bar items by date, yes, but then within the date by importance. Unfortunately, there is no native view that shows that way, so our only option is to create a custom view to do it. Here's how:

1. Click the "Arranged By:" header on the To-Do Bar.
2. Click "Custom" to launch the "Customize View: To-Do Task List" dialog box (Figure 3.2 and Figure 3.3).
3. Click the "Sort" button (Figure 3.4).

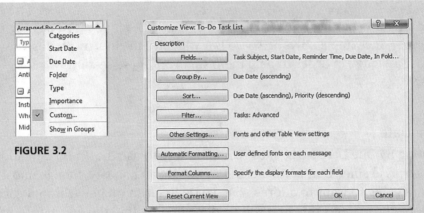

FIGURE 3.2

FIGURE 3.3

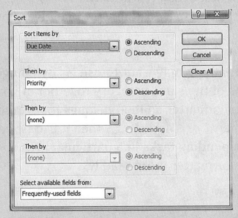

FIGURE 3.4

4. In the Sort dialog box set the Sort items by to "Due Date (Ascending)" and the Then by to "Priority (Descending)." Click OK.

5. Click the "Group By" button.

6. In the Group By box (Figure 3.5) uncheck the "Automatically group according to arrangement" box if it's checked and then set "Group items by" to "Due Date (Ascending)." Click OK.

7. Click "OK" on the Customize View dialog box. Outlook may ask you if you want to show Priority or Due Date on the view; click "No" each time.

The result is a view that looks like Figure 3.6, which is a fairly handy way to work. You'll be able to work on each item in date order, but your higher priority items will sort to the top for each date.

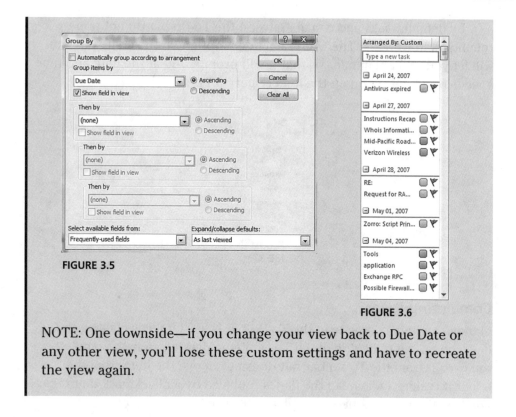

FIGURE 3.5

FIGURE 3.6

NOTE: One downside—if you change your view back to Due Date or any other view, you'll lose these custom settings and have to recreate the view again.

Adding E-mails

To flag an e-mail for follow-up and have it added to the To-Do Bar, just click the follow-up flag on the right-hand end of the message item. If you just click the flag, it sets the due date to "Today." To select a different date, right-click the flag icon and select a different date from the context menu that appears. You can even set it for follow-up on some specific future date by selecting "Custom Date" from the menu.

Adding Tasks

You can add new tasks from the To-Do Bar just by clicking the "Type a new task" field and entering the title of your new task. When you press Enter, the new task item will be added to your To-Do list for today. Unfortunately, this doesn't give you any opportunity to customize the item such as giving it a higher priority or a different due date.

To change the priority of a task item, add notes to it, or make other changes, you'll need to open it, which you can readily do by simply double-clicking on the item in the To-Do Bar.

The easiest way to change the due date of an item is to right-click the flag on the right side and select a new date from the list, or choose "Custom" to specify a date not on the list.

By default, tasks and e-mail items on the To-Do bar do not pop up reminders in Outlook. The "Add Reminder" option on the context menu will let you add a reminder so that it will prompt you at the date and time specified to take action on the item (Figure 3.7).

FIGURE 3.7

Completing Items

Marking an item complete in the To-Do bar is as simple as clicking the flag icon on the right side of the To-Do item. Marking an item complete removes it from the To-Do bar but doesn't remove the item from the folder it resides in. Instead the flag is replaced by a checkmark that tells you that the item has been completed (Figure 3.8).

FIGURE 3.8

Task Items

The Tasks folder is the primary folder for task items, and while you can work with tasks entirely on the To-Do bar without ever opening the Tasks folder, the Tasks folder does give you a much more powerful interface to work with task and even flagged e-mail items.

Creating New Task Items

To create a new Task item, press "CTRL+SHIFT+K" or click the "New" button from the Tasks folder. The new Task item Inspector will open as in Figure 3.9. You'll notice that the Task Inspector, like the other Outlook Inspector windows, does feature the Ribbon interface. One other thing I want to point out about Figure 3.9 is that it shows the Contact linking field at the bottom. That may not be on by default in yours so you may want to see Chapter 9 for an explanation of how to turn that field on.

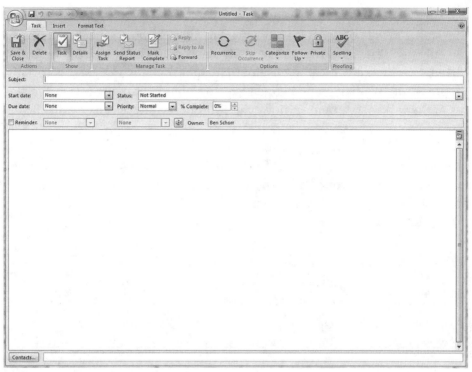

FIGURE 3.9

Subject

The first piece of information you need to fill in on the task is the "Subject," which is basically the headline or title of the task. Be as clear as you can, but not overly verbose in this field. It should tell you at a glance what the task is, but you can put any explanatory text you need in the Notes field.

Start Date

The start date is actually optional, and I usually don't use it except for large projects where I'm trying to coordinate a series of sequential, multi-day tasks.

Due Date

The due date is far more important—this is the deadline by which you want the task completed. You can type in the date, even using Natural Language dates (see Chapter 13), or you can click the drop-down arrow to see a date picker from which you can select a date. You can also omit the date if it's a task that doesn't really have any particular due date, but I discourage it. Even if you just want to pick an arbitrary date in the future, having a due date of some kind helps keep it from just stagnating, unaddressed, on your list.

Status

The status field is only marginally useful in my opinion. Typically, there are only two states in which we actually see this field: Not Started or Completed. Occasionally, it can be useful to manually change the status to "In Progress" or "Waiting on Someone Else" to remind yourself of what the status of the task is. In practice, however, I rarely see lawyers using this field.

Priority

The priority field is quite useful to let you specify how important this item is. You only have three settings here: high, normal or low. As we've seen earlier in the chapter, setting the priority can help you sort your items into a more useful order.

▼▼▼▼▼

Custom Priorities?

Sometimes we get inquiries from folks who want more than three levels of priority. While there isn't any way to add additional priorities to the Outlook Priority field, you could use the Categories field to accomplish the same thing (Figure 3.10). Simply create as many custom categories as you want by clicking Categorize | All Categories from the ribbon. In the Color Categories dialog box you can click "New" to add additional categories, which you can use to make new priorities categories. To set a particular custom priority, just assign it to the appropriate priority category. The categories sort on the list alphabetically. If you want to create a custom category that will appear at the top of the list, preface it with a symbol like "@" or ".".

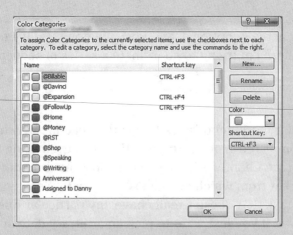

FIGURE 3.10

Percent Complete

This is a field that seems like it should be really useful, but in practice it's really pretty useless. Here you can specify how complete the task is. But is my task 45 percent complete, or is it 60 percent complete? And how much time should I waste trying to figure that out? Am I really going to reopen my Task item and change this setting every time I do 5 percent or 10 percent of my task? No. I'm going to start my task, do my task, and finish my task. In the time it would take me to try and decide if it's 65 percent complete or 70 percent complete and then open the Task item to make that change, I could probably make my task 100 percent complete.

Reminder

Reminders are one of those features that are especially interesting to deadline-driven folks like lawyers. Many firms live and die by their tickler files, and Outlook's reminders can be an effective tickler. If I want a reminder for the new task, I can check the reminder box, then specify a date and time for the reminder to occur. The time will default to the beginning of your workday, but there may be times when you want the reminder to appear later in the day. For instance, you might consider firing the reminder in the middle of the afternoon, the day before.

You can even select a particular sound file to play as the reminder. This is also a deceptively powerful tool—the sound file can be anything, including a recording of your own voice telling you something important.

Notes

The Outlook Task does provide you with an ample Notes field, which is quite handy for typing instructions, comments, or even keeping a log of the task itself. If it's a task I'm likely to do again someday, I might come in here and type "Lessons Learned" notes to myself so that next time I have to do this task or one similar I can come back to this item and read my notes.

The Notes field can also hold diagrams or pictures—sometimes I may choose to add pictures that are useful in completing the task, or hyperlinks to documents that will be related to the task.

Contacts

At the bottom of my task inspector is a field that lets me associate this task with one or more contacts (Figure 3.11). Associating the task makes it easier for me in two ways: First, I can keep track of whom I'm doing this task for, and second, when I go to that Contact item and look at the Activities Tab, I can see all of the associated task items listed right there in the Contact's activities.

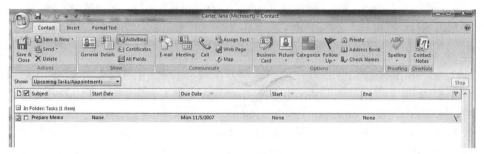

FIGURE 3.11

The Details Tab

The Details tab of an Outlook task item contains several more fields, only a couple of which are really interesting to us (Figure 3.12).

- Date Completed: This will be automatically filled in when you mark the task complete. If you manually set the Date completed, the task will be marked complete.

- Total Work/Actual Work: These would be really useful fields if they were somehow automatically tracked. Unfortunately, they're not, so they're just places where, if you want to, you can type in how much time you spent on this task. Though it seems like a natural place for an attorney to keep some informal time/billing information, the reality is that I've never seen an attorney who used these fields.

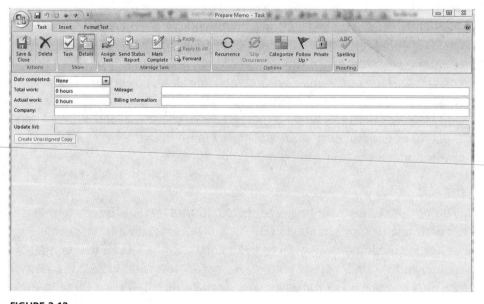

FIGURE 3.12

- Billing Information: This field I do occasionally see used—as a place to record the client/matter number this task relates to. That can be handy for the attorney who intends to bill this task later, manually.

Categorize

You can use the Categorize button to assign this task to one or more categories. The Categories feature is actually quite useful—in the Tricks chapter (Chapter 12) we'll talk about searching across all of your folders by Category as a useful way to accumulate all of the items relating to a particular category, case, or matter.

Follow-up

A task item is one of the few items where "Follow-up" is actually sort of redundant. By setting the Due Date and reminder settings, you've already set the Follow-up options and, in fact, if you were to click the Follow-Up button, you would see that it already reflects the Due Date and Reminder options you've set.

Private

If you'd like the details of this task hidden from others who have permission to view your mailbox (but not view Private items), click the Private button on the Ribbon to keep this task item to yourself (Figure 3.13).

FIGURE 3.13

Assigning a Task

After you've created your task item, you may want to assign it to a paralegal, associate, or assistant. Click "Assign Task," and the Inspector form will change somewhat to enable you to assign the task. Assigning tasks can be a very efficient way to delegate work to staff or other professionals. *And,* since Outlook will let you keep a copy of the assigned task on your own task list too, you can get almost real-time status of the assigned task, which can make it pretty easy to know which tasks are completed and which are still pending (Figure 3.14).

- The To field appears so you can select the user you wish to assign this task to. If this looks somewhat like an e-mail message, that's because that is exactly how the task will be transmitted. And yes, you can assign a task to a person outside of your organization—though there are no guarantees that person will accept it.

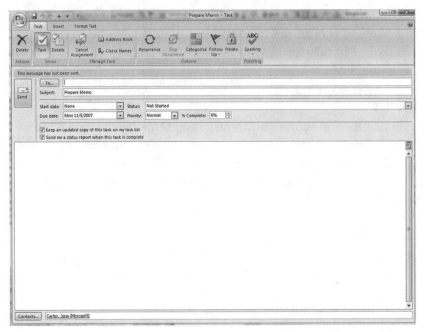

FIGURE 3.14

- **Keep an updated copy of this task on my task list:** This checkbox says that a copy of this task will stay on your task list, and as the person you assign it to updates the task—for example, marks it complete—the task will be updated on your task list as well. That can be very handy because it means that without ever even having to call and ask them, you'll know within a minute or so after the other person marks the task complete or makes some other change to it.
- **Send me a status report when this task is complete:** This setting will generate an e-mail to you indicating that the other user has marked this task complete.

Task assignment, like many features of Outlook, is actually implemented via e-mail. When you assign the task, a specially formatted RTF e-mail message is generated to the other person. When they receive it, if they are using Outlook, it will be properly rendered as a task request message. If they aren't using Outlook, it will still look like a task request message but won't have the nifty buttons allowing them to accept or reject the task, and any status update options you may have selected will have been for naught—as their e-mail client apparently doesn't support them. Task assignment doesn't require Exchange, just e-mail capability.

There are two other, not-so-obvious settings I want to suggest you consider here:

- On the Insert tab you'll find the Attach File and Attach Item buttons (Figure 3.15). If there are files in your file system or Outlook items (like an e-mail message that explains or contributes to the task) that would assist the other person in doing the task, use these to attach them to the task assignment.

FIGURE 3.15

- If there are useful Contact items in your folder that the other person might not have (the client, the expert witness, opposing counsel, or whomever), use the Business Card button to attach one or more "business cards" containing the contact information so that the other person doesn't have to bother you for that information if and when they need it.

Once you have filled out those settings, type some explanatory text in the Notes field so that the other user knows what you want them to do, and click "Send." The other person will get an e-mail message that has a Task assignment request in it. They can accept or decline that assignment—at least technically. If you're a partner and they're a paralegal, then they probably can't decline the assignment.

Recurrence

If this is a task that is going to happen over and over again, click the "Recurrence" button on the Ribbon. There are many possible patterns you can use; in fact, if the recurrence has just about any logical pattern at all, there is a way to set it through this tool (Figure 3.16):

- **Daily:** Every day? Every three days? Every weekday? Or you can have the new task regenerated some number of days after the previous iteration was completed.
- **Weekly:** Every Friday? Every other Tuesday and Thursday? Or you can have the new task regenerated some number of weeks after the previous iteration was completed. I especially see this in firms that require attorneys to review their Work in Progress reports once a week. Set up a "Review WIPs" task for every Thursday, for instance.

- **Monthly:** The 3rd of the month? The 16th of every 3rd month? The first Tuesday of every month? The last weekday of every other month? Or you can have the new task regenerate some number of months after the previous one is marked complete.

- **Yearly:** Every November 4th? The second Tuesday of May? The last day of August? Or you can have the new task regenerate some number of years after the previous one was marked complete.

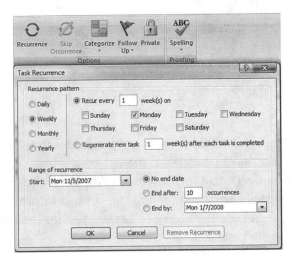

FIGURE 3.16

You can also set the range of recurrence. The start date is easy; that can be the date the first one is due. The recurrence can be endless (i.e., no end date), which is actually quite typical. We may not know at the time we create this recurrence how long it's going to go on. Or it could have a fixed number of occurrences: we're going to do this ten times or twenty times or whatnot. Or it could end by a specified date.

No matter what your recurrence pattern is, it's almost certain that you can find a way to make it work with the Outlook recurrence tool, unless the pattern is really odd or random.

Send Status Report

You may have noticed on the Ribbon a button marked "Send Status Report." That button will generate an e-mail message with the Task information below the signature block. You can type any explanatory text you wish in the e-mail and send it along to whomever you like: client, judge, co-counsel, or whomever (Figure 3.17).

FIGURE 3.17

Viewing the Tasks Folder

There are several preset views of the Tasks folder, but the Tasks folder also lends itself fairly nicely to some custom views that can aid in your productivity. Let's look first at some of the useful standard views.

Simple List

The Simple List view is just that—a simple list of every item in the Tasks folder whether completed or not. This can be an OK way to view the total-ity of your tasks, and the Search To-Do List field at the top right makes it quick and easy to find a task or set of tasks that meet a certain criteria. By clicking the headers you can sort by subject, due date, folder that the item is in, or flag status. Click the header once to sort and again to flip that sort the other way (descending instead of ascending, for instance). Notice in Figure 3.18 that this list is sorted by due date in ascending order, which places items with "None" as their due date at the top of the list. Also notice that this list includes items that are actually in many different fold-ers and not just the Tasks folder (in fact, none of the items in that screen shot are from the Tasks folder), and that's because Outlook is handling e-mail messages flagged for follow-up as if they were tasks.

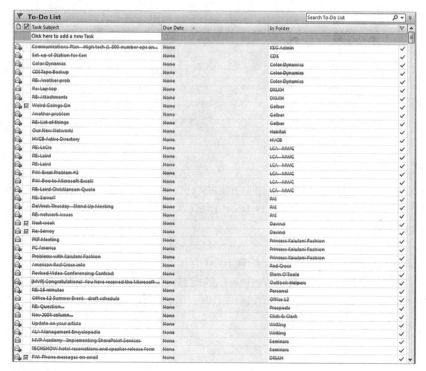

FIGURE 3.18

Detailed List

Essentially the detailed list is the same as the simple list except it adds a couple more fields.

Active Tasks

This is one of the more useful views, even though it is essentially the same as the Detailed List view except that it only shows uncompleted tasks. Active Tasks is a view that I sometimes use when I'm working through my list of open task items. Mark an item as complete, and the filter will immediately hide it from this view so that you don't have to see it (Figure 3.19).

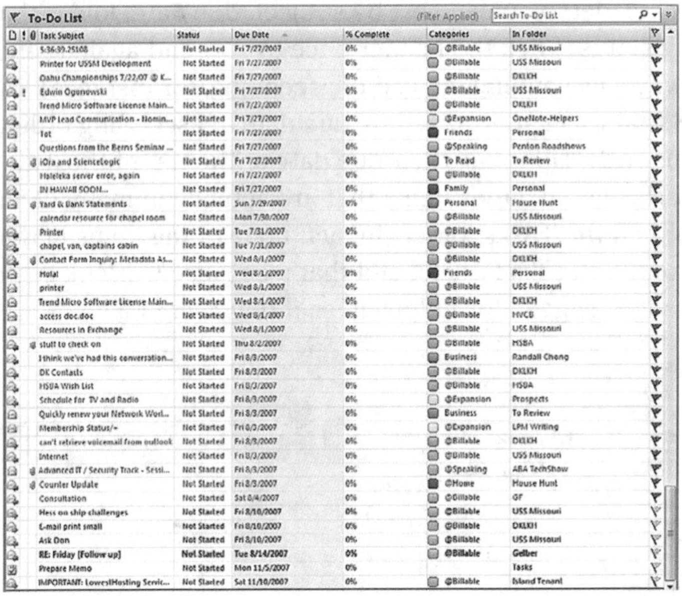

FIGURE 3.19

Next Seven Days

The Next Seven Days view is essentially the same as the Active Tasks view except that it only shows tasks (completed or uncompleted) that have due dates in the next week.

Overdue Tasks: AKA the Nagging View

This view shows you only overdue tasks. Looking to swallow your guilt and stop procrastinating? Switch to Overdue Tasks and start getting some of those items cleaned up.

Task Timeline

Task Timeline is one of those interesting views that seems like a really good idea but isn't always very useful in practice. It shows a list of your tasks, both open and completed (and with no easy way to tell the difference at a glance), along a timeline sorted by due date. It's one way to get a quick visual glance at which days you're likely to have the most (or least) tasks to do, especially if you click the "Month" button to get that view (Figure 3.20).

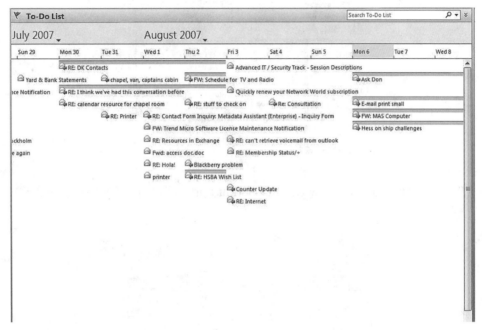

FIGURE 3.20

The To-Do List: A Custom View

The view of the Tasks folder that I use most often, however, is a custom view that I set up and find useful for helping me quickly process tasks. I'm going to take a page or two and show you how to set it up and use it, in part because I think you'll find it useful too and in part as a nice tutorial on creating and using a custom view in Outlook. In some cases it will be easier to start with one of the predefined views and just modify it, but for teaching purposes I'm going to start clean, and we'll create this view from scratch. So let's get started.

1. In the Tasks folder click View | Current View | Define Views
   (Figure 3.21).

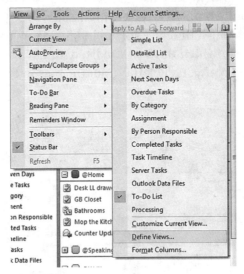

FIGURE 3.21

2. In the Custom View Organizer that appears click "New" (Figure 3.22).

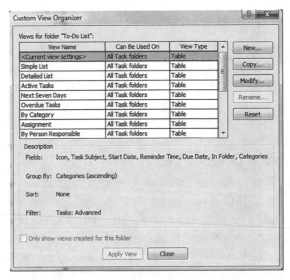

FIGURE 3.22

3. Give your view a name, I'll call mine "Get it done!" and make sure
   the "Type of view" is set to "Table." It doesn't really matter what
   you set the "Can be used on" setting to for this instance—in fact

that only matters on folders you're sharing with other folks or if you have multiple folders of this type. Just for good measure, let's set it to "All Task Folders" so that if we later create a second Tasks folder this nice custom view will be available there too.

4. On the Customize View: Get it done! dialog box, click the Fields button (Figure 3.23).

FIGURE 3.23

5. On the Show Fields dialog box (Figure 3.24) we're going to select the fields we want to show in our custom view. You'll notice that Outlook has already populated the view with a few fields for us, and it has actually done a pretty good job. The only field we're going to add is the Icon field by clicking it on the list on the left and clicking the "Add" button in the middle. Move it up so that it's listed first on the fields list. Next we're going to remove "Reminder Time" and "Due Date" (Yes, Due Date. Trust me.) Then click OK.

FIGURE 3.24

6. Click the "Group By" button on the Custom View: Get it Done! dialog, and make sure the "Automatically group according to arrangement" box is checked (Figure 3.25). Then click OK.

FIGURE 3.25

7. Click the Sort button on the Customize View: Get it Done! dialog box (Figure 3.26). Sort the items by Due Date (ascending), and set the Then By to Priority (descending). You'll notice that you can sort by up to four levels of items. If you wanted to sort by Due Date, then by Priority, then by the Contact the Task is Assigned to, and then alphabetically by Subject, you can do that. We're just going to sort by Due Date and then Priority, though. Simpler is usually better. Click OK.

FIGURE 3.26

8. Outlook will tell you that Priority is not shown in the view and ask if you want to add it. You can if you like, but I prefer not to, so I'm going to click "No."

9. Click the Filter button on the Customize View: Get it Done! dialog box. Some interesting settings are on the Tasks and More Choices tabs, but for this view what we're interested in is on the Advanced tab, so click there. Outlook may have been nice enough to create the filter we want for us—essentially we want to make sure that our custom view only shows items that are not marked complete. Since the view is going to show both task items and e-mail items, our items could be marked complete in two different ways: either the Date Completed or the Flag Completed Date could be set—the latter for tasks, the former for e-mail items that we've flagged for follow-up. We want to make sure that the view only shows items where neither of those dates exists. If those criteria aren't already set, as they are in Figure 3.27, then we'll need to set them. It's easy enough to do. Click the Field button and choose "Date/Time Fields" then select "Date Completed." It will appear in the Field field, then select the "Does not exist" condition from the Condition field, and click "Add to List." Repeat this process for Flag Completed Date by clicking the Field button again, selecting "All Mail Fields" and then "Flag Completed Date." Once the criteria have been properly selected, click "OK."

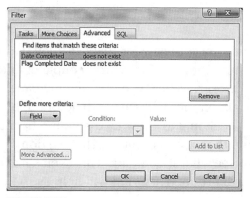

FIGURE 3.27

10. Click the Other Settings button on the Customize View: Get it Done! dialog box (Figure 3.28). We're going to leave the Column Headings and Rows section alone, but do take note

If you ever want to clear a filter from a view, come into the Customize View | Filter dialog for that view and click "Clear All," then OK your way back out.

of the "Allow in-cell editing" checkbox. This is the field that allows you to click on a piece of data on the view and change it without actually having to open the item. This can be very handy in certain views . . . but we can't use it in the view we're creating now (I'll explain shortly). We do want to Show items in Groups. Shading the group heading is a matter of personal preference, so I'll leave that to you to decide if you want to do it or not. I generally prefer not to just because I like the cleaner look of the unshaded headings.

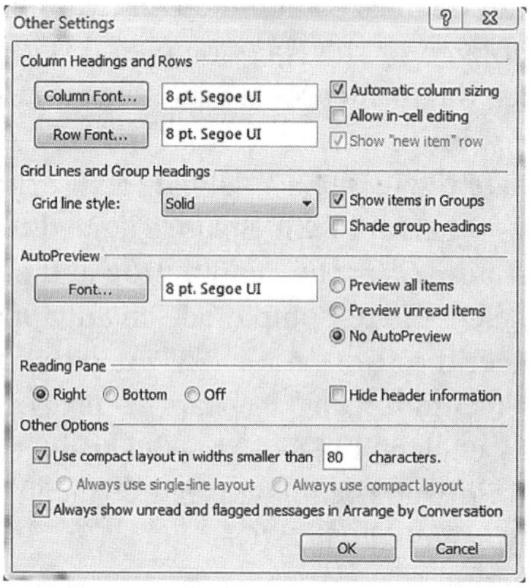

FIGURE 3.28

We will not use AutoPreview for this list—you may recall that Auto-Preview is the feature that shows the first couple of lines of the Notes field text on the list; however, we *will* use the Reading Pane. The reading pane, which I like to locate on the right side instead of the bottom, is the key to this view's utility. It's going to show us the contents of the task or e-mail item right there on the Explorer view so that we don't have to open the individual item to see what it contains. This seems like a simple thing, but it is a great boost to productivity, and will help us to be more efficient in dealing with our items.

We'll configure the view to use compact layout in widths smaller than eighty characters—even though we'll nearly always be in widths that small. The reason for that setting instead of "Always use compact layout" is so that if we do happen to turn off the Reading Pane, the display will change automatically to the single-line view, which is more efficient when you have that wide a screen to work with. The compact layout displays each entry on two lines, and any fields that don't fit will be displayed if you hover over an entry on the list with your mouse cursor.

Finally we'll leave "Always show unread and flagged messages in Arrange by Conversation" checked because we do want to show those messages. Click OK.

1. Leave Automatic Formatting and Format Columns alone. We don't need to change anything there for this view. Click OK in the Customize View: Get it Done! dialog box.

2. Apply the view (Figure 3.29).

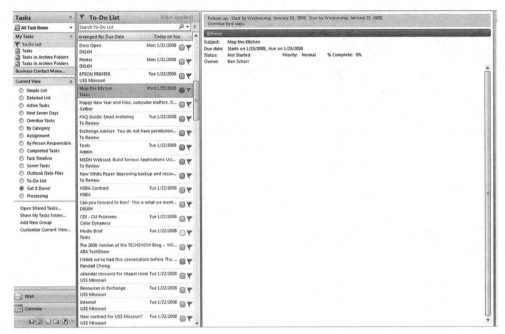

FIGURE 3.29

Now you're ready to dig in and start being productive. As you complete items, click the red follow-up flag on the right-hand end of each item, and they will disappear from this list (but not from the folder they live in).

Finding Tasks

The Tasks folder, like most of Outlook, gives you a nice search tool that will let you quickly find any tasks that you've created.

The first tool is at the top of the item list and will say, "Search To-Do List" (or "Search Tasks" if you have the Tasks folder selected). It gives you a fast, in fact almost instant, search of the current view.

To search All Task Items (which is only different because your To-Do List search may have a filter applied that restricts the search scope, like in Figure 3.31), click the "All Task Items" link on the Navigation Pane at the left.

▼▼▼▼▼

The Feature We Can't Have

One feature that I would really like to be able to add to this view is a feature I can't have without making a significant compromise to the view. I would like to be able to add the Billing Information field to the view *and* be able to enable "In-Cell Editing" so that I could click on the field right there on the list and add or edit the Billing Information for that task to make my billing easier. Unfortunately, if we turn on "In-Cell Editing," Outlook forces us into "Single Line" mode on the view. Keep that in mind when you design future views—if you want In-Cell Editing, you can't have Compact Mode.

Summary

The Tasks folder has always been somewhat unappreciated in Outlook. Users found it inconvenient at best and out of sight was out of mind. With Outlook 2007 and the filing of flagged e-mails along with task items, the Tasks folder has been reenergized as a useful and powerful tool for project and task management.

Calendaring

4

In Chapter 1 we introduced you to the Calendar module of Outlook. The practice of law is an extremely time and date intensive field of endeavor, so the Calendar is a particular favorite of lawyers.

 A man with one watch always knows what time it is. A man with two watches is never quite sure.

Arrange Your Calendar

When you first switch to the Calendar folder, you'll be presented with a view of the Calendar that shows you what is going on today. Most of your work in the Calendar will be in this Day/Week/Month view. There are several variations of this Day/Week/Month view of the Calendar, however, so let's take a minute and see the different ways in which you can look at the Calendar. Changing the way the Day/Week/Month view appears starts with clicking the Day, Week, or Month tabs at the top of the window (Figure 4.1).

Day

Day view is one of the most basic views. It shows you today, in a scheduler format, with the hours either whole or divided into thirty- or fifteen-minute increments (that is typical; if you want finer increments, keep reading). At the top of the window, you'll see the date being displayed. To change to a different date, you can click the left or right arrow buttons. Another way to control which date is displayed is to use the

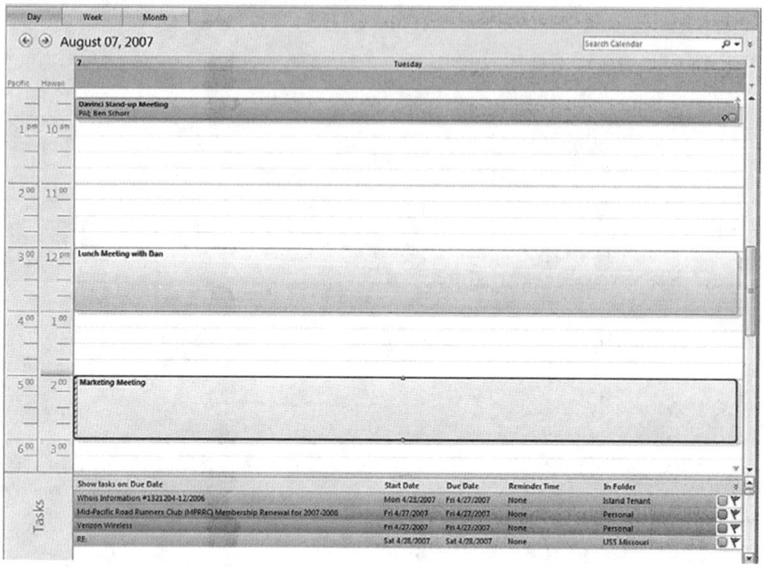

FIGURE 4.1

Date Navigator at the top left of the window. Click on the date you would like to display, and the view will change to show that date (Figure 4.2).

At the bottom of the scheduler page, you'll find one of the new features of Outlook 2007—the Calendar Task Pane has been removed and replaced by a Tasks display at the bottom of the page. This was done to address the concern that tasks didn't align well with the days they were due. Folks wanted to see their tasks on their Calendar, and to work around that, they would put tasks on the Calendar as if they were appointments.

FIGURE 4.2

▼▼▼▼▼

Tricks of the Pros

Your phone rings and it's a prospective new client who would like to arrange a meeting. "I'm pretty busy right now," she says, "but I'm available in the morning on the eleventh, in the afternoon on the thirteenth, and all day on the nineteenth or twentieth. Do any of those times work for you?"

Outlook makes it really easy to tell (Figure 4.3). In Day or Week view, click on the first date you need to see on the Date Navigator. In this case I'll click on the eleventh. Then hold down the CTRL key on the keyboard, and click on each of the other dates on the Date Navigator. Outlook will open each of the days side-by-side-by-side. Now it's easy to see and compare your schedules on those dates. When she says "OK, how about 10:00 a.m. on Wednesday the nineteenth?," you can click right on that time and type in the appointment—very efficient and effective. If you want to change the dates displayed ("Oh, wait, I'm not available on the twentieth after all, but how about the twenty-first?"), just hold down the CTRL key again, click the date you want to remove from the display, then click on the date you want to add. You can add up to about fourteen days to this view if you like, but of course the more days you add to the display the smaller they each get, so you may reach the point where the days are too narrow to be useful.

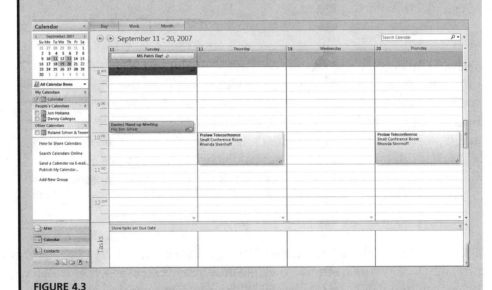

FIGURE 4.3

If you would like to see the time displayed in finer increments, you can right-click the time scale and on the context menu you can select a time increment from five minutes to sixty minutes (Figure 4.4). I generally like to set mine at fifteen minutes because I do like to keep my schedule that closely—like many attorneys, I typically bill in six-minute

FIGURE 4.4

increments—but setting my schedule much deeper than fifteen minutes results in having to scroll up and down the Calendar page more than I would like to.

Week

There are two basic variants of the Week view in Outlook: Work Week or Full Week (Figure 4.5), and you can switch between them by selecting the appropriate radio button at the top of the window. Work Week view is essentially a filtered view that omits whatever constitutes your week-end (Saturday and Sunday for most folks), and you can define your work week (if it's different from the default) under Tools | Options | Calendar Options. I generally operate in Work Week mode if only because it tends to be a slightly cleaner and clearer interface.

Month

The third basic view of the Calendar is Month view. Month view, as you probably would guess, shows you the entire month on one screen. In fact, it goes a bit further than that, showing six weeks at a time on the screen (Figure 4.6).

You can change which month is displayed by clicking the left/right arrow buttons in the header or by using the date navigator at the top left of the window. Also on the header of the month view are radio buttons that let you select what level of detail you want to see in the Month view. I leave mine set to "High" because I find that Low and Medium do not display enough information to be really useful.

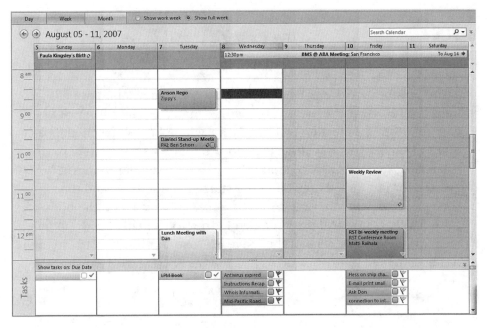

FIGURE 4.5

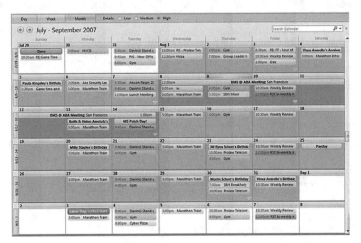

FIGURE 4.6

Adding Items

Creating new items in the Calendar is quite easy. To start a new Calendar item, just click the "New" button on the toolbar, press CTRL+SHIFT+A from any folder, or click File | New | Appointment on the menu bar. Or you can just click right on the Calendar where you want to add the appointment. Once the Calendar inspector item opens you can start to fill in the key information about the event.

▼▼▼▼▼

AutoCreate

There is another extremely handy way to create new appointment items: AutoCreate. Frequently, I receive e-mail messages from clients requesting a meeting with me or for whom I need to schedule a block of time. By simply dragging and dropping the e-mail item to the calendar group on the Navigation Pane, a new Calendar item will be created for me. I need only fill in the start and end dates and times; the subject will be inherited from the e-mail message, and the body of the e-mail message will be contained in the Notes field of the appointment item. A simple click of the "Save & Close" button, and the item has been added to my Calendar, just that easily (Figure 4.7).

FIGURE 4.7

Subject

When creating your new appointment item, the first thing you'll need to fill out is the Subject. This is the title of your appointment and is surprisingly important, as it is what will display in the To-Do Bar, on your mobile device (if you have one), on most of the Calendar views, and in any print-outs you might make. Pick a subject that elegantly describes the appoint-ment to you so that you know what it is. Don't worry about putting the location in the subject line because that information has its own home.

Location

The location field is where you can enter the physical location of the appointment if you want to. What you type here will display on most of the calendar views, on your mobile device if you have one, and elsewhere. One handy feature is that Outlook will remember the last several loca-tions you entered so that if you use the same location frequently ("South Conference Room" or "Starbucks" for instance), you can simply click the arrow at the right-hand end of the field and pick it from the list.

Start/End Time

Start and End Time are perhaps the key factors in the event. Select the start and end day of your event. They will usually be the same day (most events are just an hour or three), but occasionally they may span multiple days—for instance if you're attending the ABA TECHSHOW from Thursday through Saturday. Outlook has no difficulty with multiday events and will display them well.

Also select the start and end times of the event. Some events, like birthdays or anniversaries, have no start or end time—March 25 is Rachel's birthday, and it's her birthday all day. For those events, just click the "All Day Event" checkbox.

Recurrence

Sometimes you create a meeting that is going to happen over and over again—a "Case Status Conference" where you're going to gather your asso-ciate and paralegal in the conference room every Thursday and have the client on the phone to discuss the current status of the case, for instance. You have a bunch of options for what the recurrence pattern is in Outlook (Figure 4.8).

- Daily: Every day? Every three days? Every weekday?
- Weekly: Every Tuesday? Every other Monday and Thursday?
- Monthly: The third of the month? The sixteenth of every third month? The first Tuesday of every month? The last weekday of every other month?
- Yearly: Every November 4? The second Tuesday of May? The last day of August?

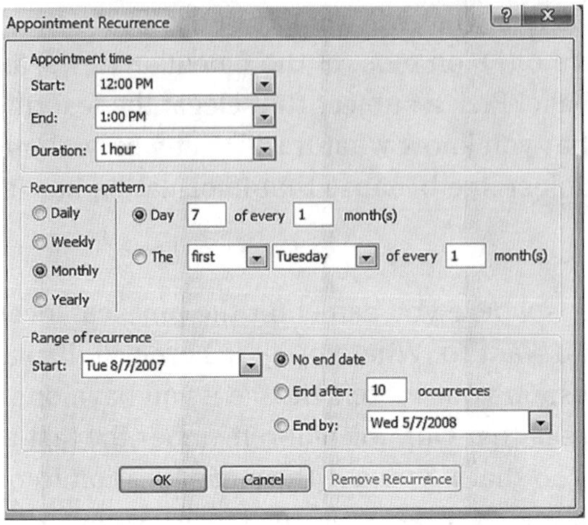

FIGURE 4.8

You can also set the range of recurrence. The start date is easy; that can be the date the first one is due. The recurrence can be endless (i.e., no end date), which is actually quite typical. We may not know at the time we set up this set of appointments how far into the future we'll be having this standing meeting. Or it could have a fixed number of occurrences: we're going to do this ten times or twenty times or whatnot. Or it could end by a specified date.

No matter what your schedule of appointments is, it's almost certain that you can find a way to make that work with the Outlook recurrence tool, unless the pattern is really odd or random.

Inviting Others

Sometimes you'll create an event to which you want to invite others. There are a few ways to do that, and which way you'll choose will probably depend (at least in part) on whether or not the others are members of your organization or are outside your organization. For folks in the same organization, the Meeting Planner is usually going to be the best way to handle it, particularly if you have an Exchange server or some other kind of central server where Calendar information is published.

Meeting Planner

If you have an Exchange server, Outlook publishes Free/Busy information, essentially your Calendar, to a public system folder where it can be used by the Meeting Planner tool to help you figure out when everybody is available to meet. To get to the Meeting Planner either click the "Scheduling" button on the Ribbon from an appointment inspector or click File | New | Meeting Request.

Finding the Best Time

The meeting planner shows you a Gantt chart, which will display the availability of any members of your organization that you specify. Under "All Attendees" on the left, enter the names of the people you're interested in having attend—one per line. Outlook will contact your Exchange server, reference the Public "Free/Busy" calendar, and return a chart that shows you what time they already have blocked out on their Calendars (Figure 4.9).

If you have a large group of people and are having a hard time finding a suitable block of time where everybody is available, use the "Autopick Next" button at the bottom left, and Outlook will immediately jump to the next point in the Calendar where all of your attendees have a long enough empty block of time to attend your meeting or event.

Once you've selected a time, filled out all the necessary appointment information, and selected all of the required and optional attendees that you want for your meeting, click the "Send" button to send invitations to all of your attendees. They will each receive an e-mail message that includes buttons for them to "Accept," "Tentative," or "Decline" your meeting invite. If they accept or tentative, then it will be placed on their Calendar for them as appropriate. They may also have the option to suggest a different time that would work better for them.

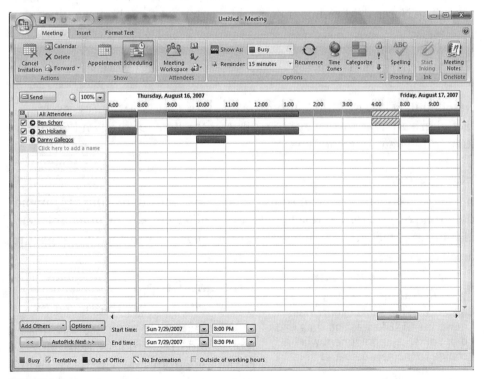

FIGURE 4.9

Two thoughts regarding the meeting planner:

1. The meeting planner is only as accurate as the data it's referring to. If your people don't do a good job of keeping their Calendars current and accurate, then you may be frustrated trying to schedule a meeting for a time that their Calendar says they're available but in reality they aren't.

2. This can be used not only to schedule people but also resources like conference rooms or projectors. To do so requires setting up the resource(s) on your Exchange server so that it/they have a Calendar to reference. Your Exchange guy should know how to do it. This is a great way to reserve and check the availability of your conference rooms without having to wait for your receptionist to get back from lunch.

Notes Field

Most people leave the Notes field on an appointment item blank, which I think is a tremendous waste. The Notes field is a very handy place to locate information about the appointment: driving directions, a proposed agenda for the meeting, notes on things you want to be sure to remember, and so forth. You can even take notes during the meeting here—either in Outlook on your laptop tablet, or using your Windows Mobile device like a Treo. The Notes field can contain a wide variety of useful information.

Rescheduling Items

Rescheduling items in the Outlook Calendar is a fairly easy process. In fact, there are two basic ways to do it: edit the item, or drag and drop the item to the new date and time.

Edit the Item

If you open an item, you can simply change the start date/time and/or end date/time on the item to reschedule it to a different date or time. You can also use this technique to make the event longer or shorter or change it to an all-day event.

▼

Want to schedule a second instance of the same event? Hold down the CTRL key as you drag and drop, and the appointment will be copied to the new date and time rather than moved.

Drag and Drop

A more effective way to reschedule or modify items is to simply use the mouse and drag/drop the item. Moving an item from 1:00 p.m. to 3:00 p.m.? Just grab the appointment item with your mouse, hold down the left mouse button, drag it to the day and time that you want it on the Calendar, and let go of the mouse button to drop it.

Don't see the day you want to move it to on the Calendar? If the time is the same ("Let's move that deposition to the twentieth at the same time"), just drag and drop the appointment to the new date on the Date Navigator. When you drop it, the Calendar view will change to that date, and you have the option to drag and drop it to a different time on that page if you like. If you're not sure which of a couple of days you might want to move the event to, or you want to look at the date first, just use the trick I shared previously; press CTRL and click on the date navigator to open the other potential date(s) alongside the date you're working with.

Sharing Your Calendar

If you have an Exchange server, sharing your Calendar with others in your organization is easy. If they just need to see when you're available, the Free/Busy service takes care of that without any action on your part. If you want to give your legal assistant more detailed access to your Calendar, for example the ability to add items for you, then you'll need to give him or her permissions to access your Calendar. Right click the Calendar folder and choose Permissions. Click "Add" to add a new user to your Calendar, and give your assistant the permission level you want (Figure 4.10).

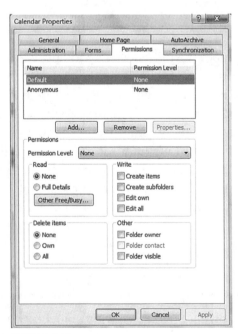

FIGURE 4.10

For most legal assistants, I find that the "Publishing Editor" role is the most effective. That allows them to add items to your Calendar, edit items, delete items—essentially to have full control over the Calendar.

▼▼▼▼▼

What About the Share My Calendar Link?

The "Share My Calendar" link on the navigation pane seems like it should be the perfect way to share your Calendar, and if you only want to grant reviewer access (read-only), then it is. But most lawyers who are sharing their Calendar want to give the person they're sharing with more thorough access, so the Share My Calendar link is insufficient.

iCalendar

iCalendar is an Internet standard for sharing Calendar information among many different personal information manager programs. Outlook 2007 supports publishing and reading iCalendar files. The easiest way to generate an iCalendar file is to use the Send a Calendar via E-mail link on the Navigation Pane that we talk about next. A .ICS file will be automatically attached to that message, which is an iCalendar file containing the calendar information you specify in the wizard.

E-mail

Outlook 2007 has added a nifty new way to apprise people of your schedule via e-mail. On the Navigation Pane (Figure 4.11) you'll find a link for "Send a Calendar via E-mail," which will generate for you an e-mail message with a very elegant HTML summary of your Calendar in it. Clicking that link will open a dialog box that lets you specify how much and what kind of Calendar information you want to include in the e-mail. If you're looking to send a quick summary of your schedule to your spouse, co-counsel, or other associate with whom you don't already share your Calendar, this can be an excellent way to let them know what you have planned (Figure 4.12).

Viewing Other People's Calendars

Like sharing your own Calendar, viewing somebody else's Calendar is far easier to do if you have an Exchange server or hosted Exchange service.

How to Share Calendars

Open a Shared Calendar...
Search Calendars Online

Share My Calendar...
Send a Calendar via E-mail...
Publish My Calendar...

Add New Group

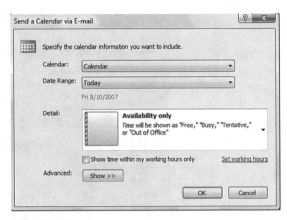

FIGURE 4.12

FIGURE 4.11

On the Navigation Pane, click the Open a Shared Calendar link, type the name of the user whose Calendar you want to open (Figure 4.13), then press Enter or click OK. If you have the appropriate permissions to open that Calendar, it'll open for you.

Can't I just open their PST file from my computer?

Not while they're using it, no. Even if you can see their PST file on a network share, PST files do not support being opened by more than one copy of Outlook at a time.

FIGURE 4.13

Printing

The Calendar folder is one of the most useful folders to print in Outlook, especially if you aren't tied to your desk all the time and don't have a PDA or SmartPhone of some kind that you can sync your Calendar with. Unfortunately, printing is one of Outlook's weak points, but there are still some valuable print formats for the Calendar.

To print a Calendar, just go to File and click Print. You can select on the Print dialog box which Calendar you want to print (the default is the currently selected Calendar), how many copies you want to print, what print style you want to print, and what date range to print (Figure 4.14).

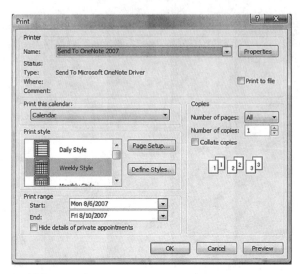

FIGURE 4.14

Pay particular attention to the date range. Generally, Outlook makes some intelligent guesses about what dates you might want to print, but I've seen a lot of instances where it doesn't print the dates you expect it to print, and the groaning attorney ends up having to toss out that wasted paper and go back to print again.

Here are a couple of my favorite print styles.

The Tri-Fold

The Tri-fold view gives you a landscaped print format that divides into three sections (see Figure 4.15):

- **Daily Schedule:** shows you your schedule for the current or selected day with hours segmented into half-hour increments.
- **Daily Tasks List:** a list of To-Do items, including e-mail items flagged for follow-up, that are due or overdue on the selected day.
- **Week at a Glance:** the schedule for the selected week.

There was a period when I didn't have a reliable PDA synchronized to my calendar so I would start each day by printing out a Tri-fold view, folding it along the dividing section lines into three panels, and then folding that down in half vertically, and sticking that in my pocket. During the day I would jot notes on the front and back of the page, including penciling in appointments or billable time on the day or week Calendars. At the end of the day, I would transcribe those notes back into Outlook or other applications (like our time and billing application) as necessary.

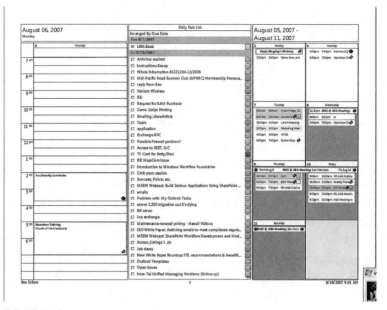

FIGURE 4.15

Weekly Style

The Weekly style gives you a nicely formatted schedule of appointment events for the selected week. This view is especially handy if you need to do event planning and arrange a schedule of events across multiple days (Figure 4.16).

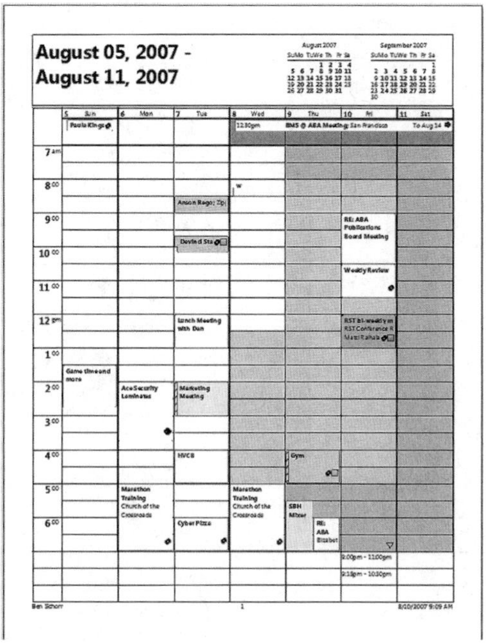

FIGURE 4.16

Calendar Details

The Calendar Details view gives you an agenda-style look at your upcoming events or appointments across whatever date range you specify.

Summary

The Calendar is an especially valuable module to lawyers and law firms as our business is a date-, time-, and deadline-oriented venture. Outlook Calendars can be shared, and you can use the Meeting Planner tool to help automate the process of finding times when everybody is available to get together. Outlook can also be used to reserve resources like conference rooms automatically. Outlook 2007's Calendar can be very effective at helping you manage your schedule and collaborate with others in your firm.

Managing Your Contacts

5

One feature that lawyers always tell me they want to use, but rarely use well, is the Contacts feature. Contacts is a complete address book that lets you keep detailed information about people and companies.

What's in a name?
A rose by any other name would smell as sweet.
—William Shakespeare

Adding Contacts

When you first open the Contacts folder, you'll find it empty, so the first thing we need to do is add a new contact item. Click the "New" button on the left-hand end of the toolbar, or click File | New (or CTRL+SHIFT+C), and the new Contact item inspector will open as in Figure 5.1.

Name and Company

The first thing to do is to enter the name of your contact and his or her company and title. None of those fields are required, though obviously you'll want to fill out at least one of those fields. When you fill out the name field, just type it as "First Last" as in "Susan Brown." Outlook will parse the field for you and decide which part is the first (or given) name and which part is the last (or family) name. It can even guess at the middle name if you enter a name or initial.

If you need to check or adjust how Outlook has allocated the names, you can click the Full Name button to get the

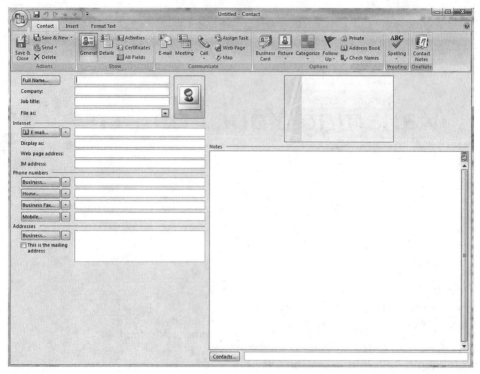

FIGURE 5.1

FIGURE 5.2

Check Full Name dialog box. Here you can change which names are placed in which fields, add a title (Mr., Mrs., Dr., etc.), or a suffix (Jr., II, etc.) (Figure 5.2).

   If Outlook has a hard time guessing at the name it will pop up the Check Full Name dialog box itself, so you can make sure it guessed right.

File As

The next field you'll have to deal with is the File As field (Figure 5.3). This field determines how the contact item will be sorted in the folder. You can file the item by first name, by last name, by company, or a combination of them. Generally, I choose between one of two formats: either "Name (Com-

FIGURE 5.3

pany)" or "Company (Name)"—the last two formats on the list. The way I decide between the two formats is actually quite simple—I simply decide how I think of that person. Do I think, "I need to call Susan Smith"? Or do I think, "I need to call Contoso Corp." Whichever I think of determines whether I file them by name first or company first.

Internet Info

The next section on the Contact inspector is for Internet info, which most often means e-mail addresses (Figure 5.4). I say *addresses,* plural, because Outlook can store up to three e-mail addresses, even though it only displays one address at a time. Click the arrow button in front of the address to choose which of the three address fields you wish to edit.

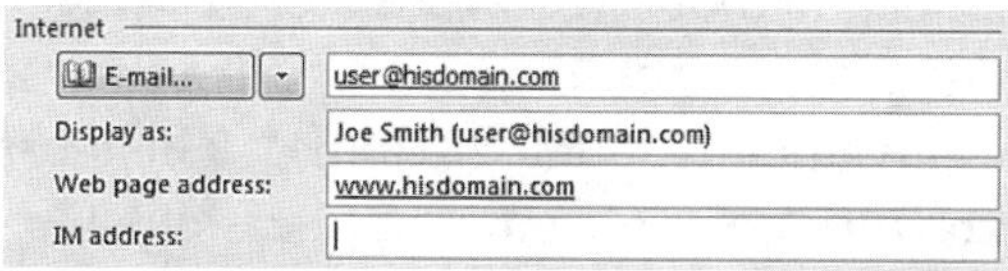

Internet	
E-mail...	user@hisdomain.com
Display as:	Joe Smith (user@hisdomain.com)
Web page address:	www.hisdomain.com
IM address:	

FIGURE 5.4

There is no advantage to picking one address field over the other; just put the first address in the "E-mail" field, the second address (if there is one) in "E-mail 2," and so forth.

You can put the contact's Web URL into the "Web page address" field and, in fact, you don't need to include the "http://" part. Just put the "www.contoso.com," and Outlook will make a hyperlink for you automatically.

Finally, if you put the user's IM (Instant Messaging) address (typically an e-mail address such as "user@hotmail.com") in the IM address field, you can be one of the relatively few people who take advantage of Outlook's integration with MSN Instant Messenger. That integration isn't especially deep—basically Outlook will simply add an icon next to their name in e-mail messages that indicates their current presence status according to MSN.

Phone Numbers

The phone numbers section is both obvious and a bit deceptive. At first glance it appears that you can enter up to four phone numbers into an

Outlook contact item, but in fact you can store up to nineteen—Outlook only displays four at a time. To change what phone number is displayed in which field, just click the arrow button in front of the field, and select which number you'd like.

When you type a phone number into a field, you don't need to include any formatting. Just type "8085551212" and Outlook will automatically convert that to "(808) 555-1212." If you're typing a phone number in your local area code, you can even omit the area code, and Outlook will add it for you (Figure 5.5).

FIGURE 5.5

Addresses

Like the phone numbers, Outlook will store more physical addresses per contact than it will display; in fact, it will store three physical addresses. The addresses are conveniently labeled "Home," "Business," and "Other," which I find tends to work great for most applications. To change which one is displayed, like with e-mail and phone numbers, just click the down-arrow button right in front of the address field (Figure 5.6).

FIGURE 5.6

When you enter the address, Outlook will make some intelligent guesses about what is the street address, what is the city, state, zip code, and even country if applicable. If you need to check or adjust what Outlook has guessed, just click the "Business" (or "Home" or "Other," depending upon which one you have displayed) button, and Outlook will display the Check Address dialog box. In this box you can adjust what Outlook thinks is the street, city, or state. Notice in Figure 5.7 how Outlook has guessed that "Rhode" is the city and "Island" is the state? This is an error we can readily correct in the Check Address dialog.

The other item I really want to point out here is the "This is the mailing address" check box. Outlook maintains a record of which of the three addresses you want to send mail to as a "mailing address," which is espe-

FIGURE 5.7

cially handy when you do mail merges (wait for it, that's coming later in this chapter), so pay attention to which address has that box checked. By default, Outlook will check that box for the first address you enter.

Notes

The Notes field is one of the underutilized features of Outlook's Contacts. This is a great place to keep miscellaneous notes on the contact—things like his favorite baseball team or what college she went to. Those seem like little things, but any good marketer can tell you that there is some value to being able to recall those little details, and while it may seem like cheating, the reality is that there are nearly 5,900 contacts in my company contacts folder, and I simply can't remember which of them was in the Peace Corps and which is an Elvis impersonator on occasional weekends.

Pictures and Other Stuff

One feature you may not even realize you have is the ability to associate a picture or photograph with a contact item. If you click the picture box as seen in Figure 5.8, which many people don't even realize is a control, you'll be given a dialog box that you can use to select the picture that will appear there. (You can also get to this by clicking the Picture button on the Ribbon).

From then on, when you receive an e-mail message from that user, in the upper right-hand corner of the message header, you'll see the picture you associated with their contact record (Figure 5.9).

There are also a number of other fields that you can store data in for an Outlook contact. On the Ribbon, there is a group called "Show," which

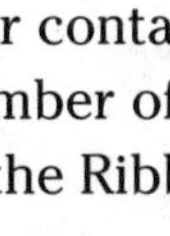

FIGURE 5.8 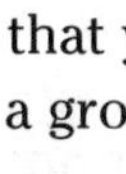   FIGURE 5.9

defaults to "General." Click on "Details," however, and you'll get another set of fields to which you can add data (Figure 5.10).

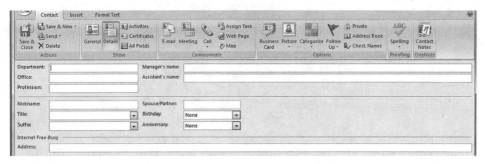

FIGURE 5.10

You will find the following among these fields:

■ **Manager's Name:** It can often be handy to note who somebody's boss is, especially if the boss is going to be the decision maker on a settlement offer.

■ **Assistant's Name:** When someone's assistant answers the phone, greet him or her by name, and you'll make a good impression.

■ **Nickname:** His name may be "Irwin," but perhaps he prefers to be called "Scooter."

■ **Spouse/Partner:** When you invite him to dinner, you can invite his spouse by name—or recall that he is a bachelor.

■ **Birthday/Anniversary:** These can be very useful to note, especially if you are in the habit of sending out a birthday/anniversary card to these folks. NOTE: When you fill out these fields, the birthday/anniversary will be automatically added to your calendar.

▼▼▼▼▼
Caution: Geek Content Ahead!

One of the other buttons you'll see on the "Show" Ribbon we just talked about is the "All Fields" button. Click on it and you'll see a fairly ugly screen, which will probably initially be blank. What you're looking at is an interface that will let you access every field in Outlook relating to this contact item. If you explore a bit, you'll discover that some of those fields are not accessible through the interface in any other way—unless you customize the form.

To begin, click the "Select From" drop-down arrow to get the list of sections you can select from (Figure 5.11). Here you'll see several categories from which you can choose, or you can just choose the "All Contact Fields" option to access the entire list.

FIGURE 5.11

Among the interesting fields you'll find here (and only here, by default) are "Children," "Language," and "Hobbies." Unfortunately, adding these files to the regular view is somewhat more difficult than you might hope. If you really want to do it, check http://www .officeforlawyers.com for tips.

If you don't want to go to the trouble of customizing and publishing the form, you can just access those fields from the All Fields view where you can edit and view them. It's just ugly and awkward.

Before you leave your contact item, there are a couple of other settings you might want to consider (Figure 5.12).

- **Categorize:** lets you assign this contact item to one or more categories. Frequently, we see lawyers who have categories for "Attorney," "Judge," "Expert Witness," and so forth so that they can more easily find and organize them. Some contacts may be members of more than one category, and that's just fine.
- **Private:** lets you hide this item in case your assistant accesses your Contacts folder, but you don't want him or her to see this particular one.

FIGURE 5.12

When you're done editing your contact item, click the "Save & Close" button on the Ribbon to add it to your Contacts folder (Figure 5.13). If you happen to click the "X" at the top right to close the item without having saved it, Outlook will prompt you to save before it closes.

FIGURE 5.13

Finding Contacts

Now that you've created your Contact item, you'll want to be able to find it again. There are several ways to do it; Outlook actually makes it quite easy to find a Contact item.

TypeTo

My favorite way of getting to a Contact item is to switch to the Contacts folder and then simply start typing the name or company. As I start to type the name, Outlook will take me right to that part of the Contacts folder. Note that what you have to type is what you've specified as the "File As"—in other words, if you have the Contact item filed as "Company, Name," then you need to start typing the Company rather than the person's name.

Search Address Books

Outlook 2007 added the Search Address Books field to the toolbar, which is available from any Outlook folder (Figure 5.14). Clicking in that field and typing part or all of the name you're looking for, then pressing "Enter" will cause Outlook to open the matching item or show you a list of items that may match for you to choose from. This can be a very quick way to get your Contact item without even having to switch to the Contacts folder. This method has the added advantage that it searches the name *and* company fields, so you don't have to recall how you filed the Contact.

FIGURE 5.14

Search Address Books also searches *all* of your defined address books and not just your personal Contacts folder. This is a great advantage if you also have a shared company Contacts folder, perhaps as an Exchange or SharePoint public folder, as a great many firms do these days.

AlphaTabs

Along the right side of the Contacts folder, you'll see the AlphaTabs that are reminiscent of the old Rolodex tabs (Figure 5.15). By clicking on a letter, Outlook will immediately take you to that part of the Contacts folder so that you can easily browse for the Contact item you're seeking.

Note that again, the File As setting becomes very important if you want to use this method for finding your Contacts—the Contacts are filed in File As order by default.

Search Contacts

If the Search Address Books field isn't quite enough, the Contacts folder has its own Search field that you can use to find your Contact items. This search field only searches the local Contacts folder, but it searches more than just name and company; you can also use it to search by city or even the Notes field in the Contact item.

Clicking the double chevrons at the right-hand end of the Search Contacts field will drop down the expanded search window that lets you

Tricks of the Pros

You can also use the Search Contacts field to search phone numbers. It's handy when a phone number you don't recognize appears on your Caller ID and you want to quickly identify the caller.

select more fields to search from or even add some of your own. Clicking the double chevrons again will collapse the window (Figure 5.16).

FIGURE 5.15   **FIGURE 5.16**

Working with Groups of Contacts

Sometimes you'll want to group your contacts together so you can work with them as a bunch. There are two basic ways to do that depending upon whether or not it's something you're going to do frequently.

Ad Hoc

If you just need to do a one-time activity with a group of contacts, you can just select the contacts and then act upon them (for example, send them an e-mail) as a group. The simplest way to do that is to simply click the first contact you want to send an e-mail message to, then hold down the CTRL key while you click each of the other contacts you wish to send your message to. If you do it properly, they'll all get highlighted, and you can then click the "New Message to Contact" icon to start an e-mail message addressed to all of those selected contacts.

Distribution Lists

If you're going to work with the same group of contacts often, you can organize them into a "Distribution List." Here's how to create a new Distribution List:

1. Click "Actions" then "New Distribution List" (or press CTRL+SHIFT+L) (Figure 5.17).

FIGURE 5.17

2. In the Name field at the top, give your Distribution List a name that makes sense. "Tennis Club" or "Jones v Smith." I often see attorneys create a distribution list for each significant matter they're working on so that when they need to send an e-mail regarding that case, they can just send it to the distribution list, which may include their associate, paralegal, client, co-counsel, and so forth.

3. Once the Distribution List is named, it's time to add members to the list (Figure 5.18). There are two types of people you can add as members of the Distribution List: those who are in your address book or those who are not in your address book.

FIGURE 5.18

a. To add somebody who is in your address book, click the "Select Members" button from the Ribbon (Figure 5.19). Your address book will open, and you can select one or more names to add to the list. There is a trick to it, however . . . after you have selected the names you want to add, you have to click the "Members" button to get them inserted into the Members field. Once you've got them in the Members field, you can click the "OK" button to add those folks to the Distribution List.

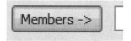

FIGURE 5.19

b. To add somebody who is *not* in your address book, click the "Add New" button (Figure 5.20). The Add New Member dialog box will appear and offer you the opportunity to enter the information for that contact. Note that there is a check box on that form that will let you also add this person to your Contacts folder if you want to, but you don't have to in order to use them in the Distribution List (Figure 5.21).

FIGURE 5.20

FIGURE 5.21

4. When you're finished adding members to your Distribution List, click "Save & Close" to save your Distribution List.

When you're ready to send e-mail to that list, just type its name (or part of its name) in the To field, and Outlook should bring it forward for you via AutoComplete. Be careful though that you get the right distribution list if you rely upon AutoComplete. It would be embarrassing at best to send an e-mail about your strategy in the *Brown v. Armstrong* matter to the *Browning v. Carter* distribution list. Take a moment to look at the name displayed in the To field before you click send.

Sharing Contacts with Others

From time to time you might want to share your Contacts with other people. Our firm shares a company Contacts folder with nearly 6,000 contact items in it. Additionally, I frequently find myself referring somebody to a friend or colleague; maybe they need a good plumber or a lawyer who can help them form an LLC. It's handy to be able to just send a quick e-mail with the contact info of that plumber or lawyer from my Contacts folder, and there are a couple of ways to do that.

vCards

A vCard is the contact version of an iCalendar item—essentially an Internet standard for exchanging contact information. It is supported by many different programs including recent versions of Outlook. To send a vCard from an Outlook Contact, select the Contact item or items then click Actions | Send Full Contact | In Internet Format. An e-mail message will be created with a .VCF file (vCard) already

Need a vCard? Create the e-mail message with the Send Full Contact technique, then just save off that .VCF file to your hard drive. You don't actually have to send the e-mail message.

attached. Simply address the e-mail message, add any explanatory text, and send it on its way (Figure 5.22).

FIGURE 5.22

Public Folders

Sharing Contacts within your firm is best done via a common server of some kind. There are two main kinds of servers you can use for that task. Which one you're likely to use depends a bit upon the size of your firm (and your budget).

Exchange

Microsoft's Exchange Server is its premier e-mail server and is commonly found in large or mid-sized firms. In addition to being a great place to host your Outlook mailbox it also has the capability to host Public Folders, which are, put simply, Outlook folders that can be accessed by multiple users. It is easy to create a public folder that is a Contacts folder where you can locate contacts you want to share with others in your firm.

Wondering if you have an Exchange server? Go to the Folder List in Outlook (Go | Folder List is an easy way), and look for one of two things:

1. Your root data store says "Mailbox-Your Name."
2. Toward the bottom of the list you see a "Public Folders" data store.

If you see those things, you have an Exchange server, and you may already have (and if not should be able to create) a public Contacts folder by following these steps:

1. Expand Public Folders.
2. Expand "All Public Folders."
3. Right-click "All Public Folders" and create a new Contacts folder.
4. Right-click your new Contacts folder, and assign any permissions you want—most law firms have at least one Contacts folder that is accessible to everyone so that they can use it as a firm-wide list of contacts.

NOTE: If it doesn't let you create the public folder, it may be that you don't have adequate permissions to create public folders. Check with your Exchange administrator, who should be able to remedy that situation quite quickly.

SharePoint

Microsoft SharePoint Server 3.0 allows you to create and work with various kinds of lists including Contact lists. Outlook 2007 lets you connect to and use those lists within Outlook as if they

---

Small Business Server

Many firms with twenty-five or fewer users have a Microsoft Small Business Server. What a surprising number of them don't realize is that Small Business Server *includes* Exchange. I have had a number of firms call to inquire about adding an e-mail server, only to have me point out that they already own one.

One of my law firm clients has an Exchange Public Contacts folder with more than 11,000 Contact items in it. Among other things, they use it to generate their annual Thanksgiving card list.

▼▼▼▼▼

Hosted Exchange

Don't have the budget for your own Exchange or Small Business Server? There are companies on the market that will give you a hosted Exchange server, which means that you subscribe to their service and they give you access over the Internet to an Exchange server. These services have their pros and cons—on the plus side, you get a lot of functionality for a lot less than the cost of deploying your own Exchange server, and you don't have to worry about managing or administering the Exchange server yourself. On the downside, you don't have as much flexibility, you're constrained by the performance (and reliability) of your Internet connection, and you're at the mercy of a third-party firm. If that firm goes out of business, then your Exchange server is gone, and your data may be gone as well.

were a regular Outlook Contacts folder. This is a nice way to share a Contacts folder throughout the firm; in fact, it's exactly how my firm does it.

The Activities Tab

On the Ribbon for your contact, you'll find a button marked "Activities." Clicking it will take you to the Activities Tab, which will show you (after a fair bit of searching) a list of recorded activities for that contact. The Activities Tab is going to show you any Journal entries or Appointments that you have associated with this Contact, as well as any e-mails that you have filed away that you have sent to or received from this contact. It's really a very useful and too often neglected feature.

Calling from Outlook

If you have your phone connected to your computer in some manner (and there are a couple of ways to do it), you can use Outlook to initiate the phone call. Select the contact you want to call and click the "Dial" button on the toolbar (it looks like a telephone handset). If you click the drop-down arrow next to the Dial button, you'll get a menu that lets you choose which phone number (assuming you have more than one saved) you want to dial, plus access to the Redial and Speed Dial menus (don't worry about

Speed Dial—in eleven years I've never seen anybody use it). If you click one of those numbers, Outlook will use the connected phone to dial the call and will give you the opportunity to initiate a Journal entry to take notes on it. When the call is over, you can click the "Hang Up" button to have the computer disconnect the call, save the Journal entry, and continue with your day. (See Figure 5.23 and Figure 5.24.)

FIGURE 5.23

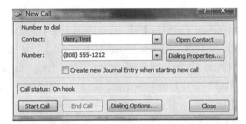

FIGURE 5.24

▼▼▼▼▼

What About Cost Recovery?

One of the potential problems with law firms using the computer to auto dial the telephone is how to collect cost recovery information for the call. Many law firms use PhoneTrak or other systems that require them to dial in a client/matter number of some sort before a call (especially a long distance call), and Outlook doesn't make an easy provision for entering that information. You may have to either collect that data manually or find some other way, perhaps with a timer in your case management system, to do that cost recovery. It's a problem that torpedoes a lot of auto dialer implementations in law firms these days.

Putting Them on the Map

On the Ribbon you'll see a button marked "Map" that does a rather clever thing: If you have a physical address specified for the contact, the Map button will open maps.msn.com, which will show you a map with the location pinpointed. You can print the map, get driving directions, or even see an aerial photograph of the location—all for free.

In some areas you can even get a real-time traffic report for the surrounding roads, in case you're planning a visit and want to see the most expeditious route to your destination.

One caveat: Naturally, you do have to be connected to the Internet at the time for this feature to work.

Sending Mail

Sending e-mail from the Contacts folder is a fairly simple matter and one that we've already alluded to earlier in this chapter. To do so, just select the Contact, or contacts, to whom you wish to send e-mail, then click the "New Message to Contact" button on the toolbar, or click Actions | Create | New Message to Contact from the menu bar. A new mail message will be initiated with the contact's e-mail address already in the To field.

NOTE: If the Contact has multiple e-mail addresses, Outlook will put *all* of them in the To field—you should decide which of the addresses you want to send to and delete the rest from the To field.

Summary

Law, like most businesses, requires interaction with a lot of different people and organizations. The Contacts folder in Outlook lets you keep track of those people and even makes it possible for you to share those contacts with other users either within or outside of your firm. Outlook's Contacts folder can be a powerful repository of information about the people and organizations you deal with in your practice. With an Exchange or SharePoint Server you can also create "public" contacts folders that you can share with your entire firm or with subgroups within your firm.

The Journal

6

The Journal is one of the underappreciated features of Outlook, especially for lawyers. The whole purpose of the Journal is to document activities, phone calls, meetings, e-mails, and so forth—seems like it should be a perfect fit for lawyers.

Creating a New Journal Entry

To create a new Journal entry, go to the Journal folder and click the "New" button on the left end of the toolbar, or just press CTRL+SHIFT+J from any folder. The new Journal Entry Inspector will open, ready for action (Figure 6.1).

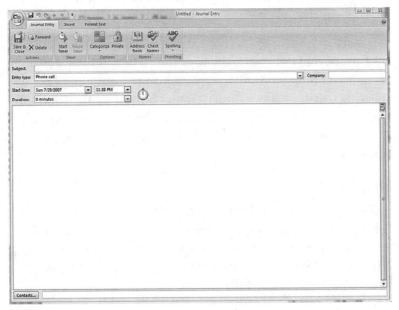

FIGURE 6.1

In the new Journal entry, type a subject and then select an Entry Type. The entry type lets you specify what kind of event it is that you're journaling and is a very useful way to organize your Journal entries. Here are some of the more useful entry types:

- **Conversation:** Useful when you want to document a conversation you just had, perhaps in the hallway.
- **Fax:** Handy for documenting a sent or received fax.
- **Meeting:** I'll often use this entry type to take notes on a meeting. Better still if you have a portable computer like a laptop or a tablet that you can take into the meeting and take notes during the meeting itself.
- **Note:** Great for random notes that you just want to quickly take and store in Outlook. Much better than the Notes folder because you have a larger space in which to type, and you can use fonts and colors and other features that the Notes folder just doesn't have. This feature also allows you to insert pictures and links to files or other items.
- **Phone Call:** This is the most common way to use the Journal; that's why Phone Call is the default entry type. Whenever my phone rings, I press CTRL+SHIFT+J before I even answer it. More on this shortly.

Once you've started your new Journal entry and selected an entry type, notice that the Journal automatically logs the date and time the entry was created. If you'd like to time the event you're journaling (like a phone call or meeting), just click the "Start Timer" button on the Ribbon. This can be a big help when it's time to bill for this event later—you can easily see what the actual elapsed time of the event was when you fill out your timesheet for billing purposes.

Taking Meetings

The Journal can be a good place to keep meeting notes, especially for ad hoc meetings that you didn't have on your Calendar. Just start a new Journal entry, choose "Meeting" as the entry type, and start the timer (if you want to). The Notes field is yours to enter your meeting notes, and the Journal will automatically record the time, date, and duration (if you started the timer).

▼▼▼▼▼
Adding Entry Types

If you want to add your own custom entry types to the Journal's list, you can, but it's not easy. It involves editing the Windows Registry, which I definitely do *not* recommend that novices do. The wrong mistake in the registry could have serious consequences for your computer. Always make sure you have a known-good backup of your system before you start editing the registry, and pay attention to what you're doing in there. Don't just go poking around with a sharp stick. OK, to add custom entry types, you need to do the following:

1. Start the registry editor. Click the Start button, click Run and type "REGEDIT," and then press Enter.
2. Go to HKEY_CURRENT_USER\Software\Microsoft\Shared Tools\Outlook\Journaling.
3. Right-click the Journaling key, and select "New" | "Key."
4. Give your new key a name.
5. Right-click your new key and choose "New" | "String Value."
6. Right-click the new string value under your new key, and rename it to "Description."
7. Double-click the new Description value you just created, and give it the name you want your entry type to appear as.
8. Repeat from Step 3 for each of the new entry types you want.
9. Close the Registry Editor.

You should now have your custom entry type(s) on the Journal list.

Logging Calls

When my phone rings, the first thing I do is press CTRL+SHIFT+J in Outlook to start a new Journal entry. It automatically records the date and time for me, and I can type any notes I need right in the entry. The other thing I want to be sure to do is to select the person who is calling or whom the call is about in the Contacts field at the bottom of the form. That way the call entry will appear on the Activities tab of the contact (see the previous chapter). If the call results in an appointment, I can drag and drop the Journal entry to the Calendar folder after I save and close it, and that will create an appointment item for me already associated with the contact with my call notes right there in the notes field of the appointment item.

Finding and Working with Journal Entries

Creating Journal entries doesn't do you much good if you can't find them later. Luckily, like most of the Outlook folders, the Journal does offer a powerful search box that will search the Journal (yes, including your notes) and bring back a list of entries that match your criteria (Figure 6.2).

FIGURE 6.2

Associating with a Contact Item

On the bottom of the Journal item, you'll find a field for Contacts. Here you can type in the name of a contact you would like to associate this Journal entry with, or you could click the Contacts button and select the contact from the list.

If you don't see the Contacts field, see page 165 for how to turn it on.

Sharing a Journal Entry with Others

There may be times when you want to share entries in your Journal with others within or outside your firm. There are a couple of good ways to do that.

Shared Journal Folder

A shared Journal folder is a little tricky to work with automatically (i.e., having your Journal entries automatically post to it), but certainly you can create a shared Journal folder and manually copy (via drag and drop) your Journal entries from your private Journal folder to the shared one for others to see. This is often useful if you want to keep case notes in a shared folder.

A shared Journal folder is going to require an Exchange server. You can create a Journal folder in your own mailbox, then right-click it, go to Properties, and give permissions to others to access it. But a better solution is to create an Exchange public folder by going to Public Folders | All Folders and creating your shared Journal folder there.

Via E-mail

If you want to just forward an individual Journal entry to somebody via e-mail, you can select that entry and click Forward from the Actions menu in the Outlook Explorer. Or just press CTRL+F if you're more keyboard friendly. That will create an e-mail item with the Journal entry attached and ready to send.

Summary

The Journal is a powerful tool for recording and tracking your activities. It's especially useful for keeping notes on phone calls or meetings and can be configured to track Office documents that you work on.

I use the Journal for any notes that I want to keep in Outlook rather than the Notes folder, which I find somewhat less than useful.

When You're Done with the Case   7

When the case is done (*Pau,* we say in Hawaii), you may not need to use the folders and subfolders you created for the case, but you'll certainly want to keep them. It's usually best to archive these folders so you can keep them without cluttering your Outlook or wasting mailbox space with them.

The first step to archiving them is to create an Outlook PST file for the items.

1. Click File | New | Outlook Data File.
2. In the New Outlook Data File dialog box (Figure 7.1), leave "Office Outlook Personal Folders File" selected and click OK. This will create a Personal Folders File in the new Unicode format that Outlook 2003 and 2007 use by default. This Unicode format is superior to the old binary format because it is far more stable with large file sizes, and it handles international

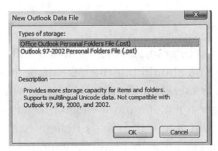

FIGURE 7.1

characters much better. On the old binary format, PST files tended to corrupt as the file size approached 2GB.

3. Give the file a name (Figure 7.2). I recommend you name it for the case or client in order to make it easier to find. Don't be shy about putting the Client-Matter number in the filename too if it makes it easier for you to find later, but remember that there are certain characters (most significantly "\" and "/") that you can't use in filenames. Also you may want to be hesitant to use periods if you don't have to. Periods will work, but the file system will take note of the period, and that can have mild consequences under certain circumstances. As a general rule, I don't use them if I don't have to. Click OK.

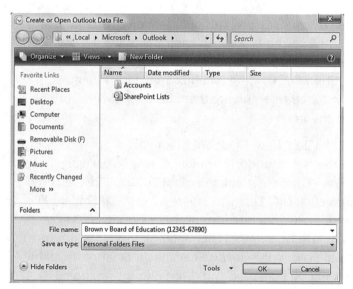

FIGURE 7.2

4. The Create Microsoft Personal Folders dialog will appear as you see in Figure 7.3. You should put the case name in the "Name" field, though this is merely a display name that will appear when you have the folder open. It's more elegant to name it properly, though, so please do give it the case or client name. A password may not be necessary but is probably a good idea. Keep in mind that there are third-party utilities to break these PST passwords, so don't rely upon them as your only means of protecting client data. Click OK.

Create Microsoft Personal Folders

File:	C:\Users\Ben\AppData\Local\Microsoft\Outlook
Name:	Personal Folders
Format:	Personal Folders File

Password

| Password: | |
| Verify Password: | |

☐ Save this password in your password list

[OK]   [Cancel]

FIGURE 7.3

The new PST file will appear on your Navigation Pane toward the bottom (Figure 7.4). Here's where adding the name in Step number 4 pays off—if you didn't put the case name in, you're just going to see "Personal Folders" listed there, and if you have multiple case files open (you can open dozens of them if you really want to) it's a lot easier to keep them straight if the display name is correct.

⊟ 🔎 Search Folders
  🔎 Categorized M.
  🔎 Containing On
  🔎 For Follow Up
  🔎 For Review
  🔎 Large Mail
  🔎 RSS
  🔎 Today (131)
  🔎 Unread Mail
⊞ 📁 Brown v Board of Ed
⊞ 📁 SharePoint Lists

✉ Mail

▦ Calendar

FIGURE 7.4

Once the file is there, expand it by clicking the [+] sign in front of it. To archive the case and matter folders, just drag and drop them from the folder where they currently exist (most likely the Inbox) to this store folder.

Calendars, Contacts, Tasks, and Journal Entries

I like to at least have a copy of all related Calendar, Contact, Task, and Journal entries for the case in the Outlook PST file just for good measure. Here's how to collect that data:

1. Right-click the case folder file you just created, and select New Folder (Figure 7.5).

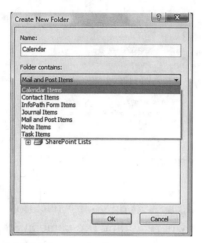

FIGURE 7.5

2. Give the new folder a name such as "Calendar," and select what kind of items the folder will contain—in this case Calendar items. Repeat these steps for Contacts, Tasks, and Journal Entries if you want to archive those as well. Click OK.

3. Open the Calendar in Outlook.

4. Search for the items relating to this case or matter. Hopefully, you used categories or typed the case or client name in the subject or body of the appointment items to make it easier.

5. In the search results, select the items you want to copy to the archive. If you want all of them, just press CTRL+A to select them all. Right-click the selected items and click "Copy."

6. Open the corresponding folder (i.e., Calendar, Contacts, etc.) in the case data file you created above.

7. Right-click in the folder and click "Paste" to paste a copy of the items into the folder. Note I said *copy* of the items. This will leave the original items in your mailbox but put a copy in the archive folder. If you want to move the items instead, you can select "Move" in Step number 5, but I generally recommend Copy for this operation.

You will probably also want to do this process for your Sent Items folder.

Long-Term Storage

Once you've archived off the e-mail folders for the case and copied the Contacts, Calendar, and Tasks items, you should right-click the case file you created and select "Close" to close it. Once it's closed, go to Windows Explorer, find that PST file, burn it to a CD, and place the CD in the hard-copy file for the case. I usually recommend making a couple of copies of the CD: one for the file, one for off-site storage, and maybe even one to return to the client. If you give a copy to the client though, be careful that there isn't anything in the Outlook data file (e-mails, Calendar items, Journal entries, etc.,) that you'd rather the client not see.

▼▼▼▼▼

As Long As You're Burning a CD . . .

There are a few other things you may want to burn to that case CD:

- Copies of any documents, spreadsheets, or other electronic files relating to the case.
- PDFs of bills or statements for the case.
- Scans of any key hardcopy documents in the case.
- Scans of any handwritten notes.
- OneNote sections.
- Any digital photos taken as part of the case.
- Sound files of any voicemails, recorded testimony, or depositions.

Summary

When the case is finished you want to gather up all of the related documents, messages, and materials and collect them all in one easy-to-store location. Outlook makes it easy to archive relevant folders, messages, appointments, and task items from within Outlook. As long as you're at it, make sure to archive electronic copies of documents and other files. CDs are an excellent archival medium, but make sure you have more than one copy and that they are properly stored for best longevity.

Using Outlook with the Rest of the Office Suite 8

Office 2007 continues the trend of integration between the various Office applications that began with Outlook 2003 and takes it to a whole new level with unprecedented integration with SharePoint.

Word

The most common integration between Outlook and Word is a mail merge from Contacts. Mail merge involves creating a document in Word that you wish to personalize with Contact information from a data source like Outlook. To do that, you'll create the document in Word, but insert merge fields instead of data in areas where you want the personalized data to appear (such as name or address). You can do that for a single letter, or you can have Word create a whole set of letters for a set of contacts.

Mail merging to Word is traditionally not nearly as easy as it should be, but Outlook 2007 improves the process somewhat. Here's how to start Mail Merge:

1. Select the contacts you want to merge, then click Tools | Mail Merge. The Mail Merge Contacts dialog box will appear. In this dialog box you have a few options you'll want to pay attention to. First, you have the Contacts setting where you can choose to have only the selected Contact items merged, or you can have all contacts in the current view merged. Note the "in the current view" part. If you have a filter

applied, only those contacts who match the filter will be merged if you select that option. In Fields to Merge, you can choose if you want to be able to select all contact fields or only the ones exposed in the current view. I generally want to see all of the contact fields, so leave that setting on the default. If you already have a merge document created, perhaps from a previous merge, select "Existing document," and browse to that file. Otherwise leave the setting at "New document." The Contact data file option allows you to create a data file from this Contacts group (Figure 8.1).

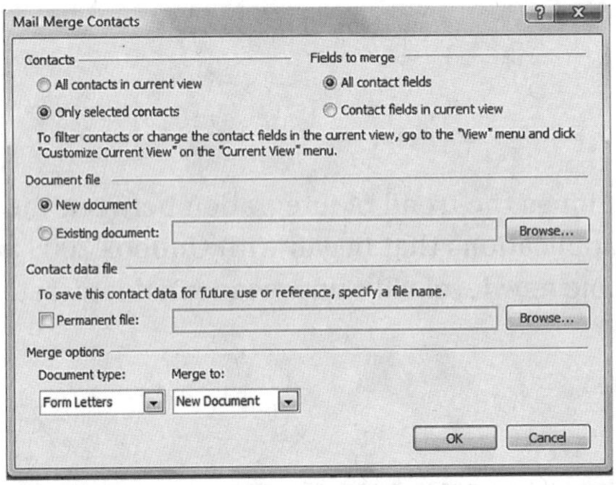

FIGURE 8.1

That can be handy if you're going to merge this group over and over again *and* if the data isn't expected to change. Generally, I prefer to work from the Contacts folder (instead of from a static list derived from the Contacts folder), so I don't use the Contact data file option. Finally, the merge options let you choose what kind of document you're merging to and where you want to perform the merge. Form Letters, Mailing Labels, and Envelopes are three very handy merges to perform. As for Merge Destination, I almost always merge to a "New Document" rather than "Printer" because I want a chance to look at the document before I actually send it to the printer. It's a waste to send the job to the printer only to find that the merge wasn't exactly what you wanted. By merging to a new document you can review the merge first and print it when you're satisfied that it's ready to go. Once you've got your options selected, click OK.

2. Word will open and give you a blank document to start with. Begin typing your document, and when you get to a place where you want to have Outlook data merged (like name), click the "Merge

FIGURE 8.2

Fields" button on the Ribbon, and a long list of possible fields will drop down (Figure 8.2). Select the field or fields you want to insert, insert them, and continue typing your document.

3. If you want to check and see how the merge is going, but aren't ready to actually run the merge yet, you can click the "Preview Results" button. You may have to click the left or right arrows to scroll left or right through the data set in order to see the data properly (Figure 8.3). When you think you're done, click the "Finish and Merge" button on the Ribbon (Figure 8.4).

FIGURE 8.3   **FIGURE 8.4**

4. For more information on Mail Merging with Word 2007, start Word, click the "Help" button on the right-hand end of the menu bar, and choose Mail Merge from the Word Help and How-To menu.

Excel

Excel is a good way to work with certain kinds of Outlook data. A common request is to sum up the duration field of a collection of Journal entries in order to use that information for billing. Here's how to do it:

1. Export the Journal items to an Excel file. Click File | Import and Export | Export to a file (Figure 8.5).

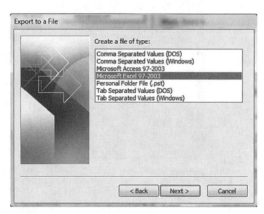

Export to a File

Create a file of type:

Comma Separated Values (DOS)
Comma Separated Values (Windows)
Microsoft Access 97-2003
Microsoft Excel 97-2003
Personal Folder File (.pst)
Tab Separated Values (DOS)
Tab Separated Values (Windows)

< Back   Next >   Cancel

FIGURE 8.5

2. In the Export to a File dialog box, select "Microsoft Excel 97-2003" and click Next (Figure 8.6).
3. Select the Journal folder from the next dialog box, then click Next (Figure 8.7).
4. Click "Browse" to select a location and name for the file, click OK, then click Next.
5. Outlook will show you a summary of actions to be performed and give you an option to Map Custom Fields (we won't for this particular merge). Click Finish. The file will be created in the location you specified.
6. Open the File in Microsoft Excel (Figure 8.8).

Here you can see the results of our basic export to Excel—I've selected the Duration field to make it stand out more easily, but otherwise I haven't customized it at all. From here it would be easy to do statistical analysis of any of the numbers or other data such as summing the duration field.

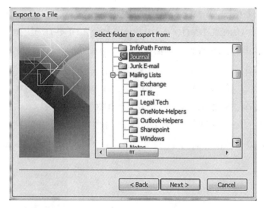

FIGURE 8.6

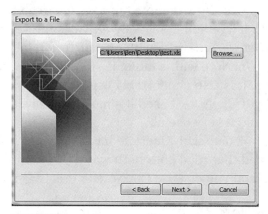

FIGURE 8.7

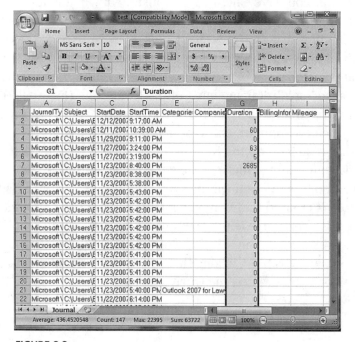

FIGURE 8.8

This is just a taste of how you might use Excel to analyze Outlook data. You can also use it to do a bulk change of e-mail addresses (for instance, if an entire company changed their domain name and you have dozens or hundreds of contact items from that company) or as a way to get Outlook Contact data into or out of some of the more esoteric programs out there. Many programs that work with data like this will allow import/export to Excel, so it can be a handy middleware to allow you to get data to or from Outlook from or to more obscure applications.

OneNote

OneNote is Microsoft's freeform note-taking software, and it is increasingly popular with lawyers. It essentially replaces the yellow legal pad as a place to create, store, and work with unstructured data like notes. While many people use OneNote with a tablet PC to take advantage of its powerful inking features, it is also comfortably useful on a desktop or laptop. In fact, when I first got OneNote, I used it almost exclusively on a desktop computer and found it very useful.

Sharing Outlook data with OneNote has gotten much more powerful in version 2007, and that road goes both ways. You can send Outlook data to OneNote, and you can use OneNote to create Outlook items.

Sending to OneNote

Outlook 2007, if you have OneNote 2007 installed, will include a Send to OneNote icon, which you can use to send the current Outlook item to OneNote. Sending an e-mail message yields a OneNote page that contains the subject of the e-mail as the title of the page, includes a header section that contains metadata about the e-mail message, and then the text of the e-mail message itself, retaining most of the formatting (Figure 8.9).

Sending Calendar items to OneNote is a slightly different process. When you open an appointment item in the inspector window, you'll find the Meeting Notes icon on the Ribbon (Figure 8.10). Clicking that will send the appointment item to OneNote. Like the e-mail message, the subject line of the appointment item will be set as the title of the page (Figure 8.11). A table is created that contains metadata about the appointment item and a large section is left at the bottom for notes.

Significantly, notice the "Link to Outlook item" link in the OneNote page, just below the table. Clicking this will open Outlook and open the item from which you created the OneNote page.

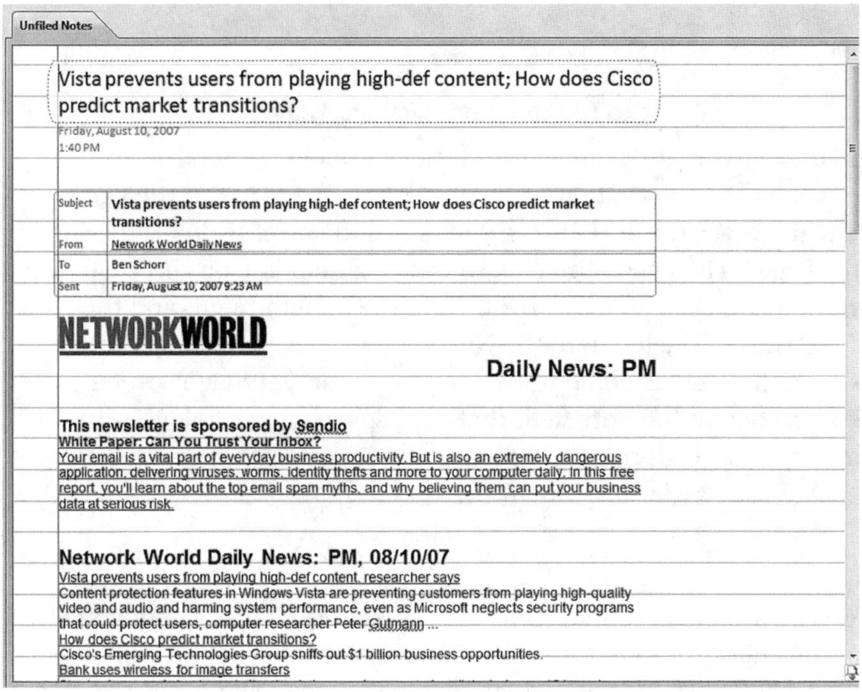

Unfiled Notes

Vista prevents users from playing high-def content; How does Cisco predict market transitions?

Friday, August 10, 2007
1:40 PM

Subject	Vista prevents users from playing high-def content; How does Cisco predict market transitions?
From	Network World Daily News
To	Ben Schorr
Sent	Friday, August 10, 2007 9:23 AM

NETWORKWORLD

Daily News: PM

This newsletter is sponsored by Sendio
White Paper: Can You Trust Your Inbox?
Your email is a vital part of everyday business productivity. But is also an extremely dangerous application, delivering viruses, worms, identity thefts and more to your computer daily. In this free report, you'll learn about the top email spam myths, and why believing them can put your business data at serious risk.

Network World Daily News: PM, 08/10/07
Vista prevents users from playing high-def content, researcher says
Content protection features in Windows Vista are preventing customers from playing high-quality video and audio and harming system performance, even as Microsoft neglects security programs that could protect users, computer researcher Peter Gutmann ...
How does Cisco predict market transitions?
Cisco's Emerging Technologies Group sniffs out $1 billion business opportunities.
Bank uses wireless for image transfers

FIGURE 8.9

Meeting
Notes
OneNote

FIGURE 8.10

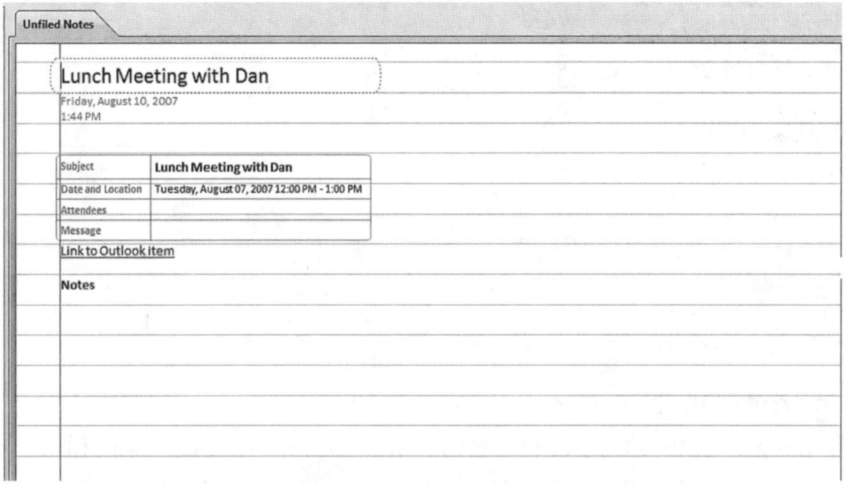

Unfiled Notes

Lunch Meeting with Dan

Friday, August 10, 2007
1:44 PM

Subject	Lunch Meeting with Dan
Date and Location	Tuesday, August 07, 2007 12:00 PM - 1:00 PM
Attendees	
Message	

Link to Outlook item

Notes

FIGURE 8.11

▼▼▼▼▼
Want to Make That Link Two-Way?

If you'd like to create a link in the Outlook appointment item that takes you to this OneNote item, right-click the page tab of the One-Note page where the appointment item is and select "Copy Hyperlink to this Page." Then click the Link to Outlook item link on the page to open the item, click in the Notes field of the appointment, and then paste (CTRL+V) the link into the Notes field. Save and close the item. This hyperlink text is going to be pretty ugly, so you might prefer to type some text in the note field that explains what the link goes to, then select that text, press CTRL+K to get the insert hyperlink dialog, and paste your hyperlink URL in there.

To send a Contact item to OneNote, select the Contact item you want to send then click the OneNote icon. The contact information will be put in a table, a link back to the original item in Outlook will be created, and a large section for notes will be available (Figure 8.12).

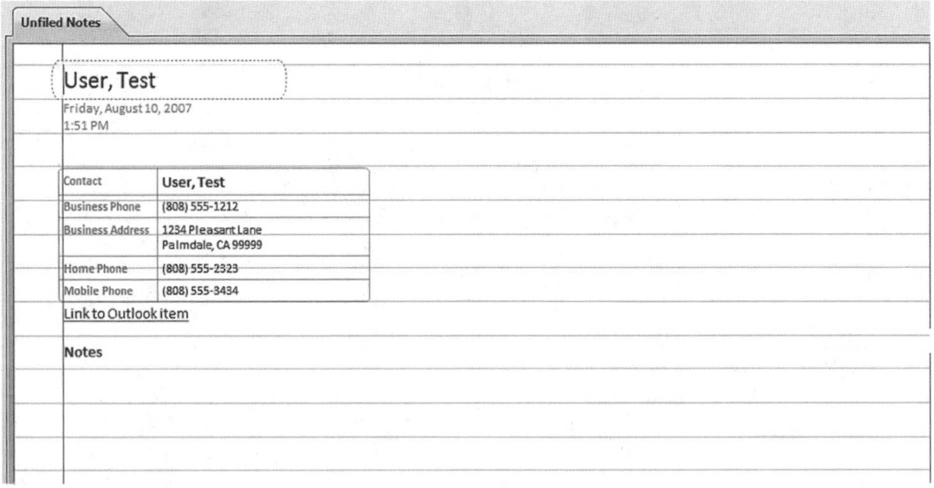

Unfiled Notes

User, Test

Friday, August 10, 2007
1:51 PM

Contact	User, Test
Business Phone	(808) 555-1212
Business Address	1234 Pleasant Lane Palmdale, CA 99999
Home Phone	(808) 555-2323
Mobile Phone	(808) 555-3434

Link to Outlook item

Notes

FIGURE 8.12

Sending from OneNote

OneNote has the ability to create Outlook items too. The best use of this feature is to add To-Do items to your tasks list (Figure 8.13). To do this, select the item in OneNote that you want to Add to the Tasks list, and click the Task button on the OneNote toolbar. You can select from a range of due dates or even mark the task complete. Especially notable about

FIGURE 8.13

this feature—if you mark the item complete in OneNote or Outlook, it will be marked complete in both. The synchronization is two-way. That's a big improvement over OneNote 2003 where you'd have to check the item complete on both sides manually.

SharePoint

Microsoft's Web collaboration server is called SharePoint. The first version of SharePoint was released in 2001 and was pretty limited in its capabilities. The second version, SharePoint 2003 (aka SharePoint 2.0) was better but in terms of its integration with Outlook still had some significant shortcomings. Notably, while you could link Outlook to SharePoint folders, there wasn't any two-way synchronization—you could *see* SharePoint items in Outlook, but you couldn't really do much with them.

The current version of SharePoint, SharePoint 3.0 and Microsoft Office SharePoint Server 2007, is another big step forward.

What Is SharePoint?

So let's look a little deeper at what SharePoint is.

Traditionally public folders have been the dominion of Exchange Server. Well, Microsoft has already laid out its roadmap for the future, and Public Folders are not part of the Exchange Plan. Yes, they're still there in Exchange 2007 and they might be there in the next version of Exchange, but that functionality is being deprecated in Exchange and moved over to SharePoint. Now that SharePoint and Outlook can bi-directionally sync, sharing the folders there makes good sense.

SharePoint consists of two elements: Windows SharePoint Services (WSS) 3.0 and Microsoft Office SharePoint Server (MOSS) 2007. Let's look at each.

Windows SharePoint Services 3.0 (WSS)

Windows SharePoint Services provides the foundation—the basic technologies that comprise the SharePoint product. It's included with Windows Server 2003, so if you have a Windows Server 2003 box, then you already have WSS—though you may not have it installed or configured. There is nothing additional to purchase for WSS.

Installing and configuring SharePoint is a subject that by itself occupies entire books, so I won't attempt to do it justice here.

To create and share contacts or calendar folders in your organization, all you need is WSS 3.0.

Independent of Outlook, WSS 3.0 also lets you create document libraries, calendars, Web parts that display traffic or weather (for example), blogs, wikis, and discussion forums. It's a powerful platform for collaboration, and since you already own it with Windows Server 2003, you should check it out if you haven't already.

Microsoft Office SharePoint Server 2007 (MOSS)

Microsoft Office SharePoint Server 2007 builds upon WSS and extends it with new capabilities. These capabilities are especially strong in the area of portals, search, and business intelligence. Since MOSS is not required for the Outlook features we're going to talk about, we don't need to worry about it here.

Calendars

One of the lists that WSS is capable of hosting is a calendar list. With Outlook 2003 and WSS 2.0 you could link to a SharePoint calendar with Outlook and synchronize the WSS calendar (or calendars) to Outlook, but it was a one-way sync only. You couldn't add or edit calendar items in Outlook and have those changes reflected in the SharePoint list. To make changes to the SharePoint calendar, you had to log into the Web interface and make your changes there. As you can imagine, this significantly limited the utility of the WSS calendars and slowed their adoption in law firms. With Outlook 2007 and WSS 3.0, that has changed and calendars can be synchronized easily between the two products.

Our firm uses a shared SharePoint calendar to list firm-wide events, holidays, meetings, and so forth.

To create a connection to Outlook, go to your SharePoint site, find the Calendar you want to connect to, click the Action menu in SharePoint, and choose "Connect to Outlook."

Contacts

The other especially useful list that WSS can host is a Contacts list. Every law firm client I have has a firm-wide list of contacts. That list includes clients, co-counsel, expert witnesses, judges, vendors, friends and family of the firm, more or less everybody the firm has contact with. Hosting those in a SharePoint list that is connected to Outlook is a handy way to work with them. Just like the Calendar folder, the Contacts folder is a two-way sync, so items can be added or edited in Outlook and will appear on the SharePoint list where either Web-based or Outlook-based users can see and work with them.

To create a connection to Outlook, go to your SharePoint site, find the Contacts folder you want to connect to, click the Action menu in SharePoint, and choose "Connect to Outlook."

Summary

Outlook 2007 can be used as a standalone product, but if you do that, you're missing out on a number of powerful collaboration features. (For additional information on collaboration tools, see *The Lawyer's Guide to Collaboration Tools and Technologies* (ABA Law Practice Management Section, 2008)).

Mail merging with Word is a great way to generate form documents, envelopes, or mailing labels easily. Excel can be used to manipulate data, perform calculations on collected data, or as a middle-step to getting data into or out of Outlook. With Outlook 2007 and SharePoint 3.0, two-way synchronization greatly increases the utility of SharePoint's folders and makes them a valuable tool for sharing information in your firm. The relationship between Outlook 2007 and OneNote 2007 has been solidified now that two-way synchronization and connectivity is possible between the products—greatly reducing the amount of effort required to use them as part of an integrated workflow system.

Managing and Maintaining 9

In this chapter, we're going to take a look under the hood at some of the settings you can use to configure Outlook 2007 to operate the way you want it to and also some of the maintenance operations Outlook occasionally requires to keep it running smoothly. Primarily, that involves backing up your data and keeping your mailbox tidy.

The Tools Menu

Most of the useful configuration settings in Outlook can be found under the Tools menu.

Options

Under the Tools menu, the Options dialog box is a goldmine of settings. Let's take some time and look at some of the settings you can configure here (Figure 9.1).

Preferences Tab

The Preferences Tab contains the basic preference settings that dictate how the various primary modules of Outlook (E-mail, Calendar, Contacts, etc.) are going to operate.

Let's look at each area one at a time.

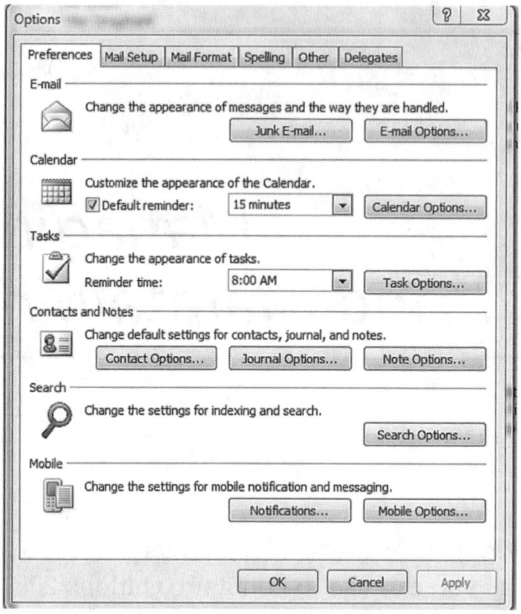

FIGURE 9.1

Junk E-mail

Outlook 2003 was the first version to incorporate a useful built-in Junk E-mail filter, and Outlook 2007 improves upon that base. The settings for it are found behind the Junk E-mail button, which generates the "Junk E-mail Options" dialog box. The first thing to look at here is the Options tab, which gives you the very important setting for the level of junk protection. I generally set this to "High," although there

> ### False Positive
>
> A false positive is a piece of e-mail that is legitimate but has been incorrectly identified as spam.

is a slight increased risk of false positives if you do that (Figure 9.2).

If you really want to lock down your account, you can set the junk e-mail level to "Safe Lists Only," but I strongly discourage that because it's going to block *all* e-mail except what you have explicitly allowed. I've never seen anybody successfully use that setting in a law firm environment.

Toward the bottom of this dialog box are four check boxes that you can use to adjust how junk e-mail operates.

- **Permanently delete suspected junk e-mail instead of moving it to the Junk E-mail folder:** If you're comfortable that no false positives are occurring and you don't want to have to keep emptying your Junk E-mail folder, you can have Outlook simply delete junk

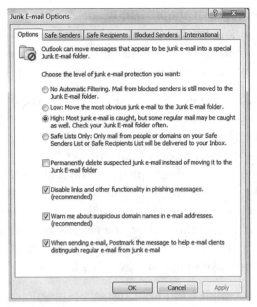

FIGURE 9.2

rather than holding it for your review. I usually do not check this
box, but you certainly can if you're comfortable with it.

- **Disable links and other functionality in phishing messages:** A
  phishing message is a message that Outlook suspects is an effort
  to fraudulently obtain personal information from you such as your
  bank account number and/or passwords. Those messages are also
  moved to the Junk E-mail folder, and, for your protection, links are
  disabled in it. I recommend leaving this box checked to reduce
  the chances that a link will be accidentally clicked in one of these
  messages.

- **Warn me about suspicious domain names in e-mail addresses:**
  Outlook can look at the e-mail address of the sender and make
  some intelligent judgments about whether the address seems suspicious. If the address is customer-service@bankofamerica.tv, that
  would seem like a suspicious address (unless Bank of America has
  moved their corporate offices to Tuavalu, I guess). I recommend
  leaving this option checked as well.

- **When sending e-mail, Postmark the message to help e-mail clients distinguish regular e-mail from junk e-mail:** Outlook 2007
  adds the Postmark capability, which adds a small electronic postmark to your outgoing message to indicate that it was personally
  generated by an Outlook client. That reduces (though doesn't
  eliminate) the chance that the message is spam, so a Microsoft
  Exchange Server or Outlook client that receives such a message

will tend to give it the benefit of the doubt when it comes time to scan for spam. In other words, this feature reduces the chance that your e-mail message will be a false positive in somebody else's spam filter. I recommend leaving this option checked.

Also on the Junk E-mail Options dialog box is the Safe Senders tab. On this tab you can add the e-mail addresses or domains of users whom you wish to make sure will get through your junk filter. You can add them manually (add the domain name without a username, such as "@rolandschorr.com," to exempt the entire domain from spam checking) or import from a file. If you want to copy or move your Safe Senders list from one machine to another, use Export to a File to export it from the master machine and then Import that list on the other machine or machines.

The following are two checkboxes at the bottom of this tab, both of which, in my opinion, you should leave checked:

- **Also trust e-mail from my Contacts:** This means anybody in your Contacts folder is automatically trusted. It's generally a safe bet that none of you Contacts are spammers.
- **Automatically add people I e-mail to the Safe Senders List:** Presumably anybody you're sending e-mail to is somebody you're willing to accept e-mail from. This adds those folks to the Safe Senders list automatically. If you decide later you don't want to automatically accept e-mail from one of them, it's easy enough to manually remove them from the list.

The Safe Recipients list seems like a curious thing—surely *you're* the recipient, so how many other safe recipients could there be?! And you don't want to just accept all mail sent to you—that would defeat the purpose of the filter! What this list actually does is allow you to accept mail that is sent to distribution or mailing lists. Your e-mail address may not be so obviously displayed. This list tells Outlook that any mail sent to that list should be accepted.

The next tab is Blocked Senders, which is not really as useful a list as it is widely perceived to be (Figure 9.3). Here, as you might guess, you can add addresses and domains of senders from whom you do *not* want to receive any e-mail. When you mark an item as *Junk* in the Inbox, the sender's address is automatically added here. Unfortunately, spammers change their e-mail addresses frequently and spoof (or fake) the address they're sending from as well. Since there are a nearly infinite number of bogus addresses from which the spammers could appear to post, trying to maintain a list of them is something of a fool's errand. You can use it, but don't waste much time on it; it's only marginally useful at best.

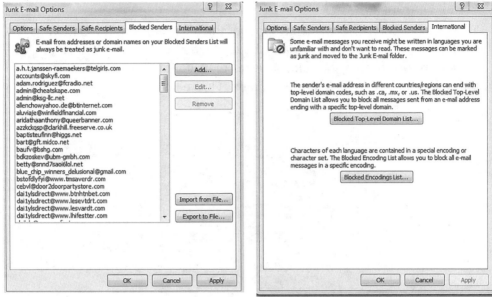

FIGURE 9.3

FIGURE 9.4

The last tab on the Junk E-mail Options is for International senders (Figure 9.4). This is actually a fairly useful new tool in Outlook 2007 since quite a lot of spam comes from countries or domains outside of the United States. There are two buttons here, and they do somewhat different things.

- **Blocked Top-Level Domain List:** The top-level domain (or TLD) is the part of the domain name on the far right. For example, in "rolandschorr.com," the top-level domain is ".com;" in "abanet .org," the top-level domain is ".org." International domains end with a two-letter country code like ".es" for Spain or ".cn" for China. If you don't want to receive any e-mail from e-mail addresses with an Estonia TLD, you can check the box next to "ee," and those messages will be blocked. Of course a spammer located in Estonia could just as easily be using a server with a .cs (Canada) or .mc (Monaco) or even .com address. But at least you block the ones who are still sending from Estonian addresses.
- **Blocked Encodings List:** Various languages require special encodings in order to properly render their special characters. If you don't care to receive messages encoded for Cyrillic or Simplified Chinese, you can block those messages here. You could even block US-ASCII, but I wouldn't recommend that unless you want to block a lot of messages sent to you in English.

E-mail Options

The E-mail Options tab controls some of the most important functions of Outlook. The E-mail Options dialog box, which results from clicking the E-mail Options button, contains a series of useful options and two useful buttons, which we'll look at individually (Figure 9.5).

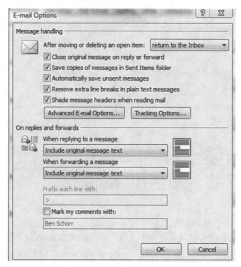

FIGURE 9.5

- **After moving or deleting an open item:** This controls what Outlook will do if you happen to delete (or move to another folder) an e-mail item that you are reading in the message

  It may say "Return to Inbox," but actually it will just return you to whatever folder you happen to have open.

  inspector. My setting, as you see in Figure 9.5, is to return me to the Inbox after each message. Other options would be to open the next message or the previous message (i.e., don't close the inspector window, just open another message in it). I have mine set to "return to the Inbox" because I actually do most of my reading and processing of messages from the Reading Pane, rather than opening the messages in an Inspector.
- **Close original message on reply or forward:** This is closely related to the previous setting and controls how Outlook will react after you've replied or forwarded a message from the inspector. Leaving the box checked will return you to the explorer window, which shows you whatever message folder you have open

(Inbox, for instance). Unchecking it will leave the message inspector open so that you can take some other action with it.

- **Save copies of messages in Sent Items folder:** Important setting for attorneys—you definitely *do* want this checked. With this item unchecked, any messages you send will just go out and disappear. In other words, while your recipient will receive it, you won't have any record of having sent it. I've never met an attorney who didn't value their Sent Items folder.
- **Automatically save unsent messages:** Outlook includes a Drafts folder, which holds messages that you have composed but not yet sent. You can manually save items to your drafts folder, or close a message you're editing without sending it and Outlook will ask you if you want to save it to Drafts, but Outlook can also be configured to automatically save to Drafts on a regular basis. (How regular? Keep reading, we'll get to that.) This is very handy, especially if your computer occasionally crashes or shuts down.
- **Remove extra line breaks in plain text messages:** This is an increasingly irrelevant setting that only really affects messages received in plain text (which fewer and fewer are in these days of HTML messages). This setting just cleans them up a bit by helping to make the formatting more readable. Leave it checked.
- **Shade message headers when reading mail:** Another setting that isn't terribly important—this just tells Outlook to make it a little easier to differentiate message headers from the message itself by the clever use of shading. Leave it checked unless you have a shading phobia.

Next let's look at the replies and forwards section (we'll get back to the buttons in a moment) as there are some useful settings to examine here:

- **"When replying to a message" and "When forwarding a message":** You have a number of options here for how you want to quote (remember, we talked about quoting in Chapter 2) the text of the message you're replying to or forwarding. You can play with the different options—the little icons on the right-hand side will attempt to give you a feel for how the setting will look—but my personal preference is for "Include original message text." That option is clean and simple—it quotes the original text, in its entirety, below your reply. Other options include the following:
  - *"Include and indent original message text"* does the same thing as "Include original message text," but as you may have surmised will add a several-character indent to the text so that the text you're quoting is set off slightly from your own.

My primary concern for that format is that adding the indent sometimes messes up the line breaks and spacing and can occasionally make the original message slightly harder to read.

- *"Attach original message"* will allow you to send a clean reply displaying only your text, but including the original message as an attachment. This is not a terrible idea for when you're forwarding a message, but it is a terrible idea when you're replying. For the most part, don't do it.

- As long as we're talking about what not to do . . . let's address the following faux pas: *"Do not include original message."* Imagine you sent somebody a postal letter in which you asked them a question. Two weeks later you received a letter back from them that said simply, "Yes." Hopefully, you remember the question you asked because their reply doesn't give you much of a clue as to what it is they are responding to. If you don't include the original message in your replies or forwards, then your recipient has to try to guess or recall what exactly it is that you're responding to.

- *"Prefix each line of the message"* is for the old school folks. Those of you who remember the old days of ASCII e-mail, bulletin boards, and newsgroups may remember when it was standard practice to prefix the text you were quoting with a character (such as ">") like this:

    > *Hi, John. How are you?*
    I'm fine, Patricia, thanks!

    Prefixing your quoted material is not a bad idea, but it's also not necessary and tends to add a lot of characters to your messages that may just make your reply look cluttered. If you do select this option, the next line will let you control what character or series of characters you want to prefix each line with.

- Finally, if you want to have your reply set off a bit more, you can choose "Mark my comments with" and have your name (or whatever phrase you like) prepended to any text you type. Also not a bad idea, especially if you're using inline quoting (remember that from Chapter 2?), but usually unnecessary.

The Advanced E-mail Options Button

Advanced E-mail Options has a lot more useful settings (Figure 9.6). The first settings in the dialog box revolve around AutoSaving messages (which you recall from just a couple pages ago) and let you specify in

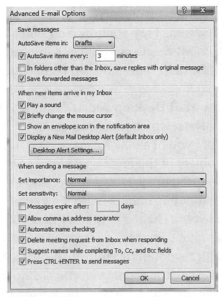

FIGURE 9.6

what folder you want to save messages, how often you want messages AutoSaved, and whether you want forwarded messages saved. The one sort of unusual option here is the rather verbose "In folders other than the Inbox, save replies with original message" option. You know an option is quirky when its description is long enough to require a comma! With this setting, if you reply to a message, your sent message will be saved in the same folder with the message you're replying to *instead* of the Sent Items folder. If you're in the habit of replying to messages in folders other than the Inbox, this can be handy, I suppose; generally, I prefer to just leave all of my sent items in the Sent Items folder.

The next set of settings control what Outlook should do when you get new mail.

- **Play a sound:** This is a real crowd favorite; just about everybody wants their system to play a sound when they get an e-mail message.
- **Briefly change the mouse cursor:** This setting is so subtle that you may not even notice it—which sort of defeats the purpose, I think. If you have this checked, your mouse cursor will change to the shape of a small envelope for just a moment when a new message is received. This is handy if you happen to be looking at your cursor at that moment and don't hear your New Mail Notification sound play. I turn off this one.
- **Show an envelope icon in the notification area:** This setting will place a small yellow envelope icon in the system tray (where the

clock is) of your screen. Since I have my toolbar auto-hidden, I can't see the System Tray anyhow, so I don't bother with this setting—I think it just needlessly clutters my tray. If you really like to have that notification that new mail has arrived, here's where you can turn it on.

- **Display a New Mail Desktop Alert:** Outlook 2003 first introduced the Desktop Alerts, which display a small rectangle on your screen to notify you of a new message. The notification shows the sender and subject of the message as well as the first sentence or so of the text (Figure 9.7). These alerts are extremely handy because, in addition to simply notifying you of the new message, they also give you a chance to quickly deal with the message. Click on the sender name, and the message will open in an inspector window so you can read it in its entirety, reply to it, forward it, move it, or whatnot. Click the red flag on the desktop alert, and you can flag it for follow-up. Is the message unnecessary? Click the black X on the lower left of the alert, and you can delete it right there and then. The alert fades in to display the message, and if you ignore it, it will fade away again after just a few seconds (click the Desktop Alert Settings button to control how long it will stay on screen). If you want to move the desktop alert to someplace else on your screen, just grab the dotted line at the top of the alert the next time one appears and drag it to the place on the screen where you want them. All subsequent desktop alerts will appear there. (I have mine appearing on the lower right quadrant of the screen.)

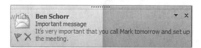

FIGURE 9.7

After you have the new mail notification settings configured, the next things to look at are the settings for sending messages. The first two settings here allow you to configure the default importance and sensitivity of the message you're composing. Outlook lets you set three importance settings (Low, Normal, High) for a message and four sensitivity settings (Normal, Personal, Private, and Confidential). It's not a good idea to change these settings by default—if every message you send goes out flagged

How Sensitive Should You Be?

Outlook has four sensitivity options, and three of them (Personal, Private, and Confidential) seem very similar. So what are the differences? Who cares? They make absolutely no difference technically—it's purely a label that has no official effect.

▼▼▼▼▼
Change the Sounds

The default sound that Windows plays when you receive an e-mail message is a rather innocuous chime, and for most people that's fine. If you'd like to change the sound played, however, just go into the Sounds applet (which you can find in Control Panel) go to the Sounds tab, select "New Mail Notification," and you can change that sound to anything you like (Figure 9.8). You can even download other sounds or music clips from the Internet—really miss your AOL "You've Got Mail!" sound? Just hit Google, and you'll find lots of sites where you can download that sound (or suitable replicas), and set that to be your new mail notification. If you have a microphone, you can even use Windows Sound Recorder (under Start | Programs | Accessories) and record your own sound to use as a new mail notification. Be careful though—whatever sound you pick is going to be heard by clients in your office, people you're talking to on the phone, and even people passing by in the hallway. It may not be a good idea to have a clip of Bart Simpson yelling "Eat my shorts!" as your office mail notification.

FIGURE 9.8

as "High" priority, people will start to ignore it. You can set any of these options on a case-by-case basis on each individual message. Use the priority or sensitivity flags selectively, and your correspondents will respect them a lot more.

Tip

Much like message recall, message expiration can't always be counted upon to remove the message from the user's mailbox.

The next setting on the dialog allows you to configure a default expiration period in days. Message expiration is a useful thing for certain messages but shouldn't be turned on by default for all messages. If you're sending a message out to the entire firm to tell them that there are bagels in the lounge, then it's nice to set that message to expire at the end of the day. The bagels themselves will certainly be expired by then, and anybody who doesn't read that message until the day after tomorrow isn't going to care that there were bagels in the lounge today. By setting the message to expire after a day or two, you helpfully allow that message to be automatically removed from their Inbox after the specified period of time (if it is still unread).

The next several options are all quite useful, and I recommend you do check them.

- **Allow comma as address separator:** Somewhat obviously, this setting allows you to use a comma to separate multiple addresses in a To, CC, or BCC field. If this box is unchecked, you'll have to use a semicolon to separate the addresses. With the box checked, you can use either a comma or a semicolon.

- **Automatic name checking:** When you type a name in the To field (instead of an address), Outlook will automatically check that name against your e-mail address books (typically your Contacts folder) and automatically substitute the e-mail address for that contact if it can. This is the AutoResolve feature we talked about in Chapter 2, and it's very helpful.

- **Delete meeting request from Inbox when responding:** This setting seems a little out of place here (for reasons I'll explain momentarily), but it's a useful one. Once you have responded to a meeting request, it will have been either discarded or added to your calendar as appropriate. There's rarely any reason to keep the request message.

- **Suggest names while completing To, CC, and BCC fields:** This is the AutoSuggest feature we talked about in Chapter 2 and is at least as handy as AutoResolve. With this feature, when you start to type a name or address, Outlook will pop up a list of addresses you've used that match that text. In Chapter 12 we'll talk about how you can clean up that list if there are addresses on it you don't want (Figure 9.9).

- **Press CTRL+Enter to send messages:** For you keyboard fanatics (see Chapter 13) this is a useful setting because it gives you

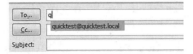

FIGURE 9.9

a fairly easy way to send your messages when you're ready. CTRL+Enter will act the same as ALT+S or clicking the "Send" key. Some of the older e-mail applications used "CTRL+Enter" for send, so if that's what you're used to, you'll like this.

Tracking Options

The second button on the E-mail Options dialog that we want to talk about is the Tracking Options button (Figure 9.10). The options available through this dialog are all related to how Outlook is going to handle special messages like meeting requests and receipts. It seems like this would have been a more logical place to put the option to delete meeting requests after processing, but somehow the Outlook team didn't see it that way at the time.

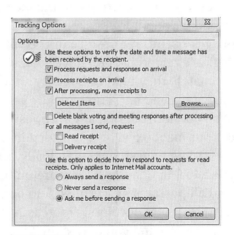

FIGURE 9.10

- **Process requests and responses on arrival:** This tells Outlook that if a response or request is received, it should do whatever automatic processing it can do without requiring user action. In Chapter 4 we talked about meeting requests and responses—in short, this means if you get invited to a meeting or if somebody responds to your invitation to a meeting, assignment of a task, or voting buttons, Outlook will record that response automatically for you. This does not mean that Outlook will automatically accept meeting requests for you; you'll still need to handle those yourself. There *is* a way to tell Outlook to automatically process meeting requests, but we'll get to that shortly.

- **Process receipts on arrival:** This setting does essentially the same thing that the previous setting does except in this case for delivery and read receipts.

- **After processing, move receipts to:** Typically, this is "Deleted Items," meaning that after the receipt is processed, it should be deleted. If for some reason you want to keep the receipts, you can disable this setting or change the folder to something else. Perhaps you would want to create a "receipts" folder that would be your repository for those items. I'm not a big fan of sending receipt requests, so you've probably already figured out that I'm not going to be a big fan of keeping them either.

- **Delete blank voting and meeting responses after processing:** Voting and meeting responses are never truly blank. What this setting means is that the other party has responded but not typed any text. They have undoubtedly clicked a voting button or accepted/declined your meeting request. Outlook will process that vote or response and then delete the message from the Inbox. I do recommend leaving this checked.

- **For all messages I send, request (read receipt/delivery receipt):** These settings are tempting and I have seen some attorneys use them, but ultimately they tend to be fairly annoying. Imagine if every message you send out automatically generates *two* messages back to you, not counting any response the other person might send. Your mailbox will get crowded in a hurry with messages that are, to be honest, only marginally useful. (See: "Would You Like a Receipt" in Chapter 2 for more on this topic). You wouldn't send all postal mail "certified," so don't automatically generate receipts. It just needlessly increases the amount of message traffic on the Net and can even sometimes annoy your correspondents. There may be individual messages where you would want to request the receipt, and in Chapter 2 I showed you how to do that if you want to.

The final section on this dialog involves how Outlook should handle read receipt requests and is part of the reason why read receipt requests are only marginally useful: Some of your correspondents will be able to refuse to send you one, which defeats the purpose of the receipt. Note that this only works on Internet Mail (essentially POP and IMAP) accounts. If you have an Exchange server, Exchange will take care of sending the receipts, and it's not as easy to prevent them.

Calendar

The first option you'll see for the Calendar is a feature that was widely requested in previous versions of Outlook and that is the ability to set (or disable) the default reminder. Out of the box Outlook will remind you of new appointment items fifteen minutes before the start time. You can change that (or turn it off) to anything from five minutes to two weeks.

Want an unusual default reminder time? You're not limited to what you can choose from the drop down—just click in the field and type whatever you want; "23 minutes" works just fine.

Under the Calendar Options button is the Calendar Options dialog box, which gives you access to several useful configuration settings for the Outlook calendar. Let's take a tour of that dialog box and see what we can do with it (Figure 9.11).

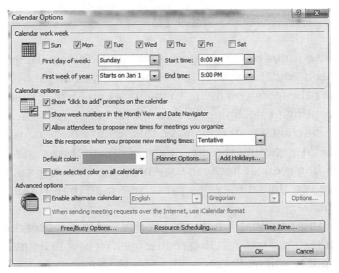

FIGURE 9.11

- **Calendar work week:** One of the handy Outlook views relates to showing you just the "Work Week" instead of the full week. Here you can specify your work week. If you're an associate, it's probably Monday through Saturday. If you're a partner? Monday through Thursday but with Wednesday off for golf. This same section lets you specify what day of the week starts your week (for most folks it's Sunday). If you prefer to have the start of the week as Tuesday or something else, you can set it here. You can also specify what constitutes your workday (8:00 a.m. to 5:00 p.m.? 6:00 a.m. to 6:00 p.m.?).

- **Show "click to add" prompts on the calendar:** One side benefit of writing this book is that it has caused me to review my settings on this machine, and I realized that I had left this feature enabled. All "click to add" does is show you a little prompt when you hover over a particular time on the calendar. After the second time you've done it, you really don't need the reminder anymore, so I usually turn it off.

■ **Show week numbers in the Month View and Date Navigator:** If you really like to know what the week number is (1–52), you can turn on this option, and Outlook will show the week numbers on the left side of the Date Navigator (yes, on the To-Do Bar as well) (Figure 9.12).

FIGURE 9.12

■ **Allow attendees to propose new times for meetings you organize:** If you are especially democratic, you might be willing to let the folks you invite to meetings go further than simply accepting or declining; you can let them propose new times for the meeting. I generally leave this feature on because I think it expedites getting the meeting scheduled. If they decline your meeting request because they have a scheduling conflict, it will save you time if they can propose a time that works better for them.

■ **Use this response when you propose new meeting times:** When you respond to a meeting request with a new meeting time, your response will be flagged with one of three acceptance levels: Tentative, Accept, or Decline. Accept is a little forward in my opinion; it implies that the other person will be OK with your proposed change. Decline is a little antisocial; it says, "Meet when I want to meet or else I'm taking my gavel and going home!" Tentative is the default and really the most diplomatic of the three options, in my opinion.

■ **Default color:** Outlook 2007 lets you configure what color you would like the Calendar to be by default. This is purely a visual setting with personal preference. It's followed by a checkbox that lets you configure if you want that color applied to all calendars you have or just to your default calendar.

Before we move on to the Advanced Options section, let's stop to look at the Planner Options and Add Holidays buttons.

Planner Options

Planner Options lets you fine-tune how the meeting planner and group schedule will work (Figure 9.13). Notably, it will let you configure if calendar details (such as the subject and location of the person's appointment) will be shown on the grid or if hovering over part of the grid will show the details. Note that any appointment marked private will *not* show details on the grid regardless of the settings here.

FIGURE 9.13

Add Holidays

Add Holidays is a fairly simple tool; it lets you add holidays for different regions, nations, or cultures to your calendar (Figure 9.14). If you want to add the national holidays of Argentina or the Jewish religious holidays to the calendar, just go in to the Add Holidays tool, check the appropriate box from the many listed, and click "OK."

FIGURE 9.14

The Advanced Options section of the Calendar Options dialog box contains some rather esoteric settings that few attorneys are really going to use, but let's take a quick look at them nonetheless:

- **Enable alternate calendar:** If you want or need to see what the current date is on the Hebrew calendar or the Chinese zodiac calendar, you can enable that here and the date will be shown in both the English and the alternate calendar as in Figure 9.15.

⊙ ⊙ 丁亥年 August 05, 2007   **FIGURE 9.15**

Adding Other Special Dates

There are several sites like www.calendar-updates.com that provide downloadable calendars you can add to your Outlook calendar for things like your favorite baseball team's schedule, lunar schedules, and other dates like that to further enhance (and clutter) your Outlook calendar. Never miss another Chargers game or eclipse!

- **When sending meeting requests over the Internet, use iCalendar format:** The iCalendar format is an open standard that can be understood by several different calendaring programs in addition to Outlook 2007, including Apple's iCal, Lotus Notes, and Novell's Groupwise (among others). This setting is handy if you're interoperating with users who use one of these alternate e-mail programs, and you want to be able to send them meeting requests that they can work with in a somewhat automated fashion.

Free/Busy Options

The meeting planner in Outlook (see Chapter 4) relies upon the published Free/Busy information in order to populate the grid and let you know when users are available to meet. Under the Free/Busy Options button is the Free/Busy Options dialog box (Figure 9.16), which lets you configure some of the settings around how your schedule will be published. The top section of this dialog box is generally more important than the lower section. Here you can control how many months of data you want to publish and how often you want it updated. If people are trying to schedule a meeting with you for three months in advance, you have to be sure you have published at least three months worth of data. It may be tempting to set these

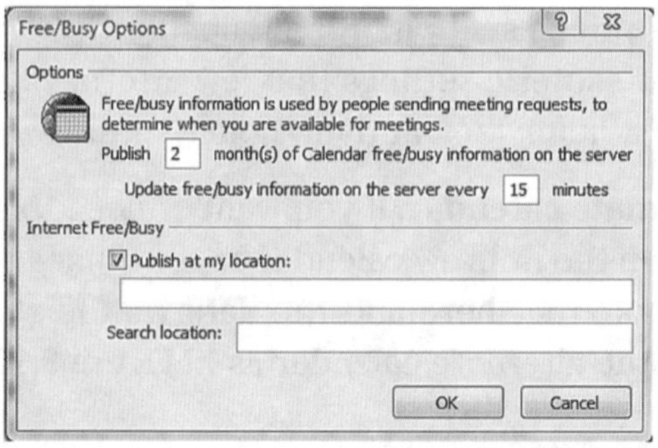

FIGURE 9.16

▼▼▼▼▼
Caution: Geek Content Ahead!

The iCalendar format is defined by RFC (Request for Comment) 2445 and is intended to facilitate sharing of calendar information among many different calendaring and personal information programs. iCalendar files typically have either an .ICS (for an appointment item) or a .IFB (for free/busy information) file extension. While they are often exchanged via e-mail, you can also share iCalendar files in many other ways, such as publishing them on a Web site. Is your firm hosting an informational seminar? In addition to advertising it on your Web site, why not create an iCalendar .ICS file that people can download from your Web site so that they can automatically add your seminar to their calendars quite easily!

to twelve months and two minutes, but resist that temptation—you'll add a lot of unnecessary traffic to your network, and most people really don't need quite that level of Free/Busy information. Every fifteen minutes is usually perfectly sufficient, and two months ahead is usually enough as well.

If you happen to be one of the few lawyers using Internet Free/Busy, you can configure whatever server you would like to have your Free/Busy information published to as well as whatever server you would like to search to see other users' Free/Busy information.

Resource Scheduling

The Resource Scheduling dialog box lets you configure automatic processing for meeting requests (Figure 9.17). Generally, these settings are only used on resource mailboxes—that is, mailboxes created for conference rooms or other resources in order to maintain a calendar for those resources. If the conference room or other resource has its own calendar,

FIGURE 9.17

its free/busy information will be published, which means that you can reserve that resource via the Meeting Planner in Outlook. (Go back to Chapter 4 for more details on this.)

In the Resource Scheduling dialog box, you configure Outlook to automatically accept meeting requests as long as they are not conflicting (which means as long as something isn't already on the calendar for that date/time). If you are doing this for a resource calendar (as opposed to your personal calendar), make sure to click the "Set Permissions" button to give permission to those users in your firm who need to view and edit the calendar.

Time Zone

The Time Zone dialog box lets you configure which time zone(s) Outlook displays on the calendar (Figure 9.18). You can give it a label, select the time zone from the list, and specify if you want Outlook to adjust for daylight savings time. Most people show just a single time zone on their calendar. If you deal a lot with a location in another time zone, you may want to add it as an "additional time zone" here. The result, as you can see in Figure 9.19, is that both time zones will be shown side by side on your calendar. It's very handy for helping you calculate what time it is in that other zone right now.

I want to mention two other buttons on the Time Zone dialog box:

■ **Change Calendar Time Zone:** Outlook 2007 keeps track of what time zone an appointment or meeting was created for and will maintain that information even if you change the time zone on your computer. When I travel, I typically change the time zone on my laptop to reflect the time zone I'm currently in. Be a little

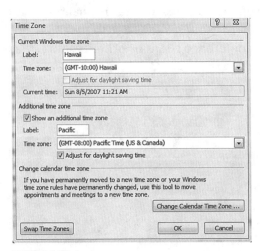

FIGURE 9.18

FIGURE 9.19

careful with this one. If you just change the time zone Outlook displays, it will *not* change your appointments to the new time zone, even though they might display correctly adjusted for the time zone. If you change time zones long term, perhaps because you've transferred to a new firm or office someplace else, then you can click this button after you've changed the time zone, and all meetings and appointments *will* be changed to the current time zone. Time zones in Outlook can be especially tricky, and they were the cause of a lot of complaints and concerns in earlier versions. Outlook 2007's keeping better track of the time zones is a good step, and this button will undoubtedly help matters, but I'm still a little wary of messing around with the time zone settings for appointments, so please exercise caution before you click this button. If you do happen to click it accidentally, you should be able to undo the damage by changing the Outlook time zone back to your native time zone and clicking the Change Calendar Time Zone button again.

- **Swap Time Zones:** This just changes your primary and secondary time zones. It's handy if you're travelling from your primary time zone to your secondary and just want to quickly swap them. This doesn't alter any of your data, so it's safe to do and undo.

Tasks

The next section of the Options dialog box lets you control some of the Task settings. Right off the bat you'll see a familiar option: Default Reminder Time. This is the time of day that Outlook is going to pop up the first reminder about tasks due that day. The option to turn reminders on or off by default is located under the Task Options button, as we'll see in just a moment.

Click the Task Options button to get the Task Options dialog box like you see in Figure 9.20.

- **Overdue and Completed task colors:** Somewhat self-explanatory, here you can specify how you want Outlook to display tasks that are overdue or marked completed. I usually recommend that you leave these alone unless you really want your completed tasks to appear listed in green or something.
- **Keep updated copies of assigned tasks on my task list:** This controls what Outlook will do with tasks you've assigned to other people (see Chapter 3). When this is checked, tasks you assign will stay on your task list, and when the other party marks the task complete, it will automatically show as completed on your task list as well.
- **Send status reports when assigned tasks are completed:** This option will generate an e-mail message to the person who assigned you a task informing them that (and when) you marked it complete. This is actually a fairly handy feature, so I tend to leave it enabled. In some cases it can save you having to manually notify the person who assigned the task.
- **Set reminders on tasks with due dates:** This setting controls whether Outlook will default to setting a reminder on all tasks that have due dates (which most tasks should). Personally, I only want to be reminded of the truly important tasks, so I have this option turned off. If you want to be reminded of all of your tasks, you can turn it on.

Contacts

The Contacts Options dialog contains a couple of useful settings relating to how the contacts are filed and also for turning on a very useful feature in other folders.

- **Select the order you want Outlook to use for new names:** This setting controls how Outlook is going to interpret a name you type in (Figure 9.21). The default, which is the most sensible for most folks, is "First (Middle) Last," which means if you type in two names, it will be interpreted as "First Last," but if you type in three, the second one will be assumed to be the "Middle" name. If you never type in middle names but do have the occasional contact with two last names, you could change the format to "First Last1 Last2."

FIGURE 9.21

- **Check for duplicate contacts:** This is one of the more important settings in Options, I think. I've seen users who end up with many duplicate contacts in their folder, especially if they have numerous contacts and tend to lose track of which contacts they already have. By having Outlook check for duplicates, you can significantly reduce the incidence where you have multiple contact items for the same person.
- **Show Contact Linking on all Forms:** If you're using Outlook the way I encourage you to, you will make sure that this setting is turned *on*. This is what enables the field in Journal, Calendar, and other items so that you can link the items to their related contact or contacts.
- **Show an additional Contacts Index:** This setting deals with the alpha tabs on the right side of the Contacts folder. If you want to have an additional set of characters there such as Greek, Cyrillic, Vietnamese, or others, you can check the box and select the additional character set you'd like to see.

Journal Options

The Journal options are primarily centered on automatically recording items for various activities or contacts. You can specify on the left side what activities you want automatically recorded and on the right side which contacts you want to record them for (Figure 9.22).

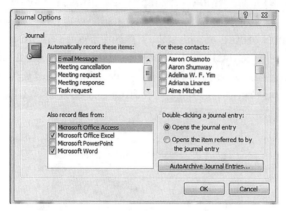

FIGURE 9.22

One problem with this dialog box is that there isn't any easy way to select all contacts; in fact, selecting contacts basically involves scrolling down the list and individually checking those contacts you want monitored.

Clicking the "AutoArchive Journal Entries" button simply opens the AutoArchive settings for the default Journal folder. You can get to the same place by right-clicking the Journal folder, choosing Properties, and going to the AutoArchive tab. We're going to talk more about Archiving in just a few pages—it is one of the better tools Outlook offers for keeping your mailbox lean and clean (Figure 9.23).

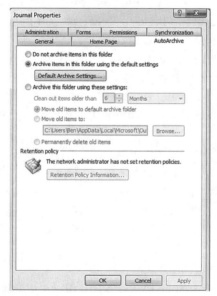

FIGURE 9.23

Notes Options

Like the Notes themselves, the Notes Options offer very little of substance. Here you can set the default color (yellow) and size (medium) of the Notes as well as the default font used. Those are roughly all the options you can set—which is just as well because that's roughly all of the features that the Notes folder offers anyhow.

Search Options

One of the best new features of Outlook 2007 is the powerful new Instant Search capability that makes it possible to find almost any item within moments (Figure 9.24). The Search Options help us to tune and configure how Search is going to work.

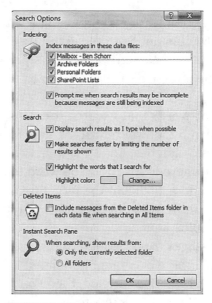

FIGURE 9.24

- **Index messages in these data files:** This is where you can specify which data stores you want to index. For the most part, you'll want to index everything, but I can envision a scenario where you might have a data store you don't care to search.
- **Prompt me when search results may be incomplete because messages are still being indexed:** When you do a search while the Indexer has items it hasn't finished reading yet, you may not get a complete set of results. If you have this box checked, Outlook will tell you that it's still in the process of indexing so that you know that there may be more items that match your query but which Instant Search can't yet return to you.

- **Display search results as I type when possible:** When you type into the search box in Outlook, it will show you results as quickly as it can; often the first results will appear as you're typing in the search. As you type more and more of your query, some results will be removed as they don't match your search and others will be added as the search continues. This is a useful setting, and I recommend you leave it enabled.

- **Make searches faster by limiting the number of results shown:** This setting is something of a mixed bag. With it on, only 100 results will be displayed for your search, and if what you wanted was the 101st result, then you're out of luck. With it off, you may see more results, but the search can take considerably longer—consider if you run a rather basic search against a store of 50,000 items such that 5,000 items are returned as matches. That search could take quite a while, even with the new Windows Desktop Instant Search capabilities. I recommend you leave this option enabled. Frankly, it's pretty rare that any of us will have the patience to scroll down to the 218th search result anyhow.

- **Highlight the words that I search for:** This is another good setting. The search tool will return the item that contains the word or phrase that matches, but if the item is quite large, it may be hard to find where in that item the word or phrase is contained. By letting Outlook highlight the target text, you can make it considerably easier to pick out that word or phrase from within a large or complex item.

- **Include messages from Deleted Items:** I see no reason to enable this setting. If there is content in Deleted Items that you want indexed and regularly searched, then you need to hurry up and read Chapter 11. The Deleted Items folder is your trash can, and you wouldn't keep an inventory of the contents of your trash can, would you?

- **When searching, show results from:** The default is "Only the currently selected folder," which makes the most sense. When you run a search, it is easy to have Outlook search all folders—most of your searches will probably involve items in the current folder, and there's no sense wasting time searching across all of your folders if you just want an item in the current folder. Leave this setting on ". . . currently selected folder" unless you have a compelling reason to change it.

Mail Setup Tab

The Mail Setup Tab is primarily concerned with configuring the accounts Outlook will work with and the data files it will use to store your data. These settings are part of the user profile, which can be configured from the Mail applet in Control Panel.

Before we get into the content behind the buttons, let's take a look at the settings we can configure right from the Mail Setup tab (Figure 9.25).

Under Send/Receive, the "Send immediately when connected" check-box defines whether clicking "Send" really sends the message or whether it merely places it in the Outbox where it will wait for you to send it manually. For the most part I like to send immediately, but if you're the type who is so careful you proofread the photocopies, then I can see where you might want to have the extra step of sending manually from the Outbox as just another safeguard against accidental, or premature, transmission.

If you're still using dial-up . . . well, then you really need to talk to a broadband provider in your area. With so much legal research and other tools available to you online these days, it's almost malpractice, in my opinion, to practice law without a high-speed Internet connection. That said, if you're a lawyer who still uses a dial-up connection, you can use

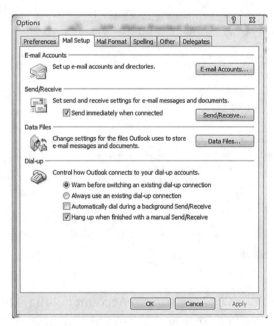

FIGURE 9.25

the dial-up section to control how Outlook handles your modem connection. The most notable options here concern whether Outlook will automatically dial your connection, if it's not already connected, when a background send/receive is scheduled. (We'll talk about background send/receive in just a few moments). The second useful option here is the one that tells Outlook to hang up the dial-up connection when you're finished with a manually initiated send/receive (which happens when you click the Send/Receive button). You may want to uncheck this button if you're accustomed to leaving your dial-up connection connected and don't want Outlook disconnecting it for you.

E-mail Accounts

The E-mail Accounts dialog is large and important (Figure 9.26). Here's where you configure the various kinds of services that Outlook is going to work with. First and foremost is the e-mail accounts tab, which lets you specify which e-mail accounts you want Outlook to send and receive on. To add a new e-mail account, just click the "New" button and work through the wizard, which will help you add the account.

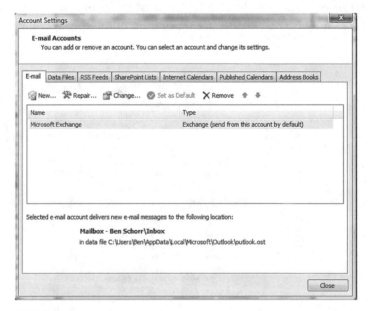

FIGURE 9.26

New to Outlook 2007 is the Auto Account Setup (Figure 9.27), which will take your e-mail address and password and attempt to configure your server settings for you. It does an admirable job in most cases, and in those instances where it can't manage, it will give you the chance to configure that account manually—like our ancestors did.

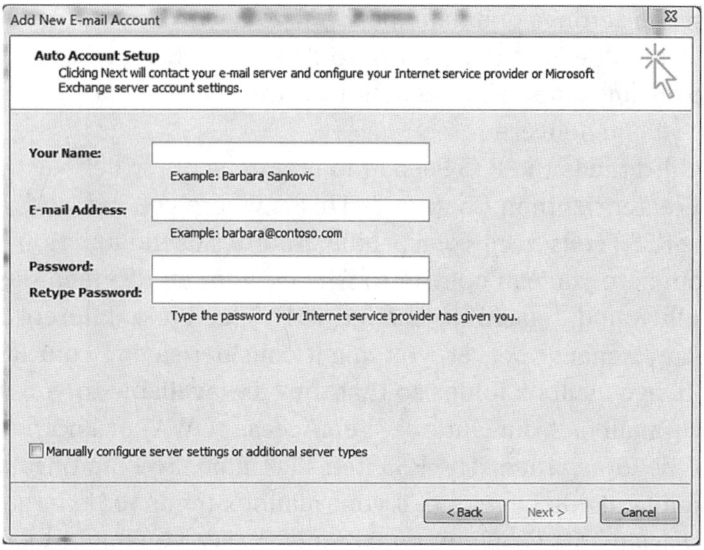

FIGURE 9.27

If you're having problems with your account, the Auto Account Setup even provides the facility to try and repair the account by resetting the account settings and password—just select the account and click "Repair" from the toolbar.

Once the account is set up, if you want to make changes to it, just select the account from the list and click "Change."

The second tab you'll find in Account Settings relates to data files— where the items are going to be stored (Figure 9.28). From this tab you can add a new data file (generally a "Personal Folders File" or PST file),

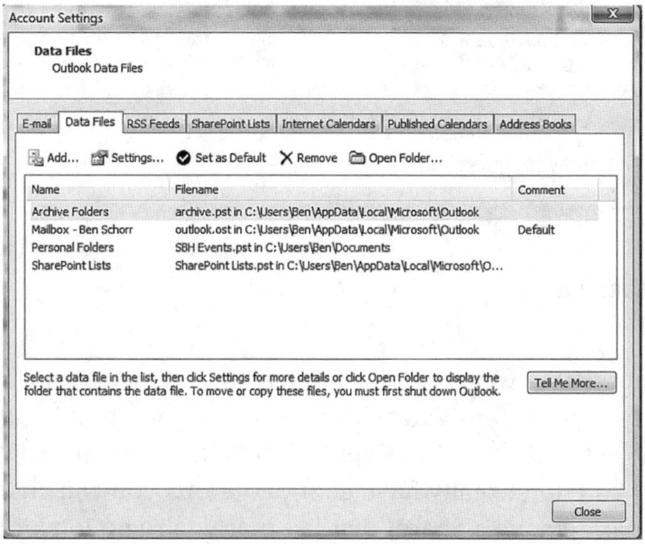

FIGURE 9.28

can adjust the settings of a data file, remove one from your profile (which does *not* delete the file from your hard drive), or change which data file is set as the default. The default data file is where new e-mail messages will be delivered.

The third tab is the RSS Feeds tab (Figure 9.29), which we talked about in greater depth in Chapter 2. This is where you can add, change, or remove RSS Feeds from your profile. Another useful function of this tab is that from here you can control to which folder an RSS feed posts. I've occasionally found it useful to change an RSS feed to a different folder. If you have an Exchange server, you might consider saving your RSS Feeds to an Exchange mailbox folder so that they are available to you if you check your mailbox from Outlook Web Access (OWA) or another computer, but be forewarned: The RSS items are going to count against your mailbox quota, if you have one. If your mailbox tends to be large and bumps up against its size limit on a regular basis, you might look to see if you can move your RSS feeds off to a personal folders file on the hard drive—so you don't have to fill the limited mailbox space with RSS items.

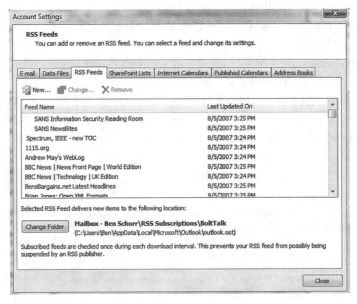

FIGURE 9.29

As I mentioned in Chapter 8, Outlook 2007 and SharePoint 3.0 give you the ability to do two-way synchronization of SharePoint lists, and that's the subject of the fourth tab in the Outlook Account Settings dialog (Figure 9.30). You don't really have a lot of options you can change on this tab, but you can remove a SharePoint list that you're no longer interested in synchronizing with Outlook.

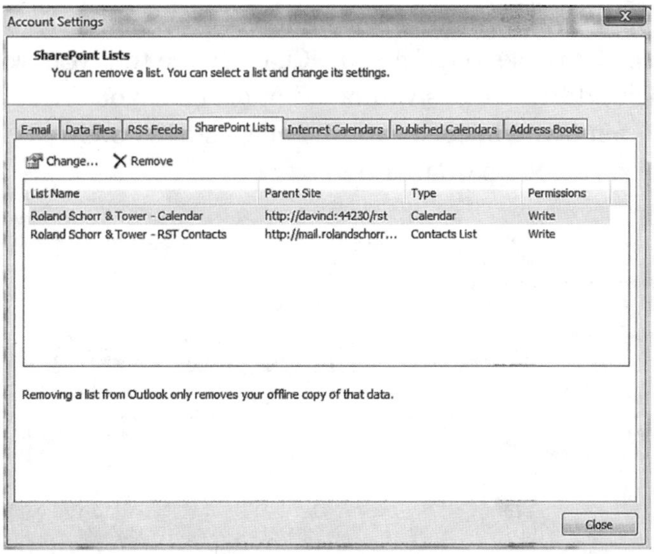

FIGURE 9.30

The next two tabs are Internet Calendars and Published Calendars, which are concerned with calendars published to the Internet that you might subscribe to (or publish). The settings here are relatively self-explanatory, and in my experience very few attorneys use these features.

▼▼▼▼▼

Important!

If you have an Exchange server mailbox, *do not* use a Personal Folders file as your default message store. Don't do it. There are a lot of reasons not to, but some of the better reasons include performance, reliability, and resiliency. Most Personal Folders files are stored on the local hard drive of the computer, and few local hard drives are backed up. When your hard drive on your computer dies (not if, *when*), it will take your Personal Folders file with it; and if you don't have a backup, then you just lost all of your e-mail, contacts, calendar, and other Outlook data. I know what you're thinking: "I'll just put my PST file on a network drive! Then it'll get backed up." Locating the default PST file on a network drive is *not* a supported configuration, though. Yes, it does work for some people. But most networks have too much latency, and that can cause performance issues and can cause corruption issues with Outlook PST files. It's OK to locate a PST file that gets only occasional access on a network share, but *not* your default data store that is going to be sending and receiving mail on a frequent basis.

The last tab is very useful, however. It lets you configure your Directories and Address Books (Figure 9.31). Chances are that you won't be adding any new address books without support from your IT department or consultant, but if you needed to add a new address book, such as an LDAP directory, you could do that here.

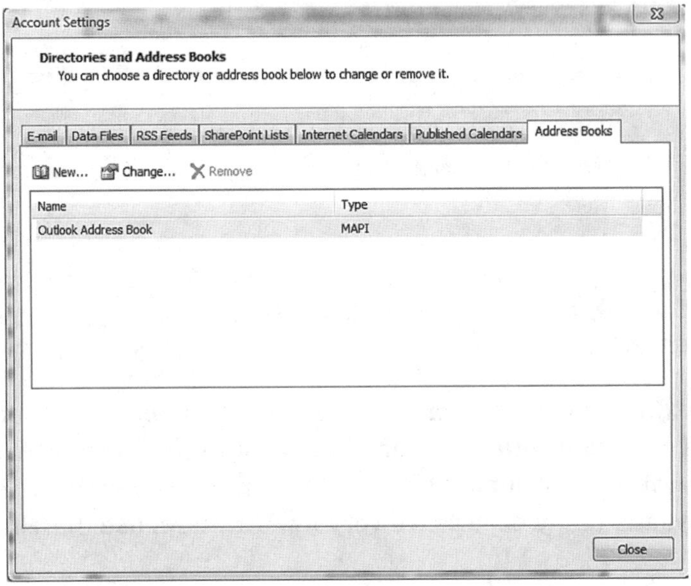

FIGURE 9.31

More likely you'll be checking on the health and configuration of your Outlook Address book here (Figure 9.32). The Outlook Address Book is what you see when you click the "To" button on a new e-mail message and what gets checked when you type a name into the To field and AutoResolve tries to find the e-mail address. The Outlook Address Book is typically comprised of your organization's Global Address List (if you have one) and any Outlook Contacts folders (including Public Contacts folders

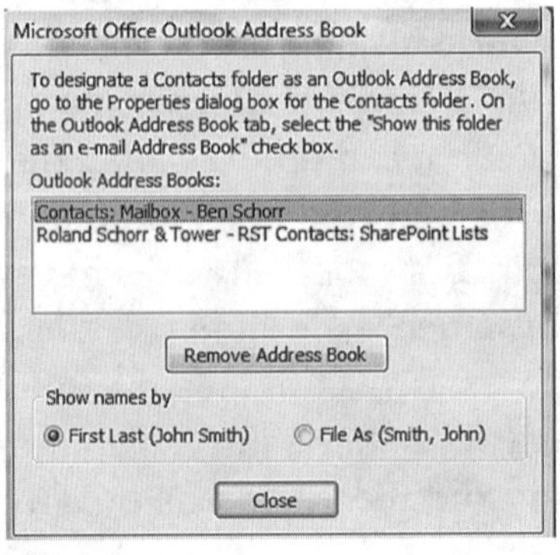

FIGURE 9.32

or SharePoint Contact lists) that you have defined. Select the Outlook Address Book and click the "Change" button, and you'll see a list of the Outlook Address Books you have configured. If there's one you don't want to use anymore, you can remove it from here. If there's one that you *do* want to use, but it doesn't appear here, then you know that you have to add it. To add a Contacts folder to the Outlook Address Book, just right-click the Contacts folder you want to add in the Outlook Explorer window, select the Outlook Address Book tab, and check the box for "Show this folder as an e-mail Address Book."

Send/Receive

If you're working with multiple e-mail accounts, it can be very handy to define Send/Receive Groups that control which accounts get checked automatically for mail and how often. You can define multiple send/receive groups or put all of your accounts into a single group if you like (Figure 9.33).

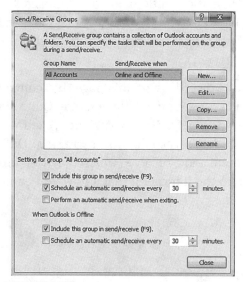

FIGURE 9.33

The following are some of the basic settings you can apply to groups:

- **Include this group in send/receive (F9):** This means that if you press F9 (or click Tools | Send/Receive | Send/Receive All) to initiate a manual send/receive operation, this group will get checked as well.
- **Schedule an automatic send/receive every . . . :** This lets you tell Outlook to do a background send/receive on a timed schedule. Background send/receive means that Outlook will send any

---

Wait a Minute Mr. Postman

People love to get e-mail, and I've watched users sit there and press F9 every twenty seconds in the hopes that some little nugget of wonder will have arrived in the last moment. Generally, it's not a good idea to check a POP3 account more often than every five minutes. You want to let your last check finish before your next check begins, and if you *do* have messages to download, it may take a couple of minutes to finish. Be patient.

---

messages in the Outbox and download any waiting messages in the background, automatically, without the user having to manage or monitor the process. In fact, the user is rarely aware the Background send/receive is occurring (hence the term *Background*) unless new mail is received during it. Please note the sidebar to the left that advises it's not wise to set this lower than five minutes. If you really need your e-mail constantly updated and instantaneous, invest in an Exchange server.

- **Perform an automatic send/receive when exiting:** This is the "Last one out turn out the lights" setting. It basically says that when you're exiting Outlook, before it closes it will do one final send/receive to make sure that any messages in the Outbox are sent (and, of course, one last slight hope that an e-mailed wonder may have arrived).

There are also two settings on this page that control how Outlook will behave when it's operating in Offline mode. Quite simply, they control if this particular Send/Receive Group will be checked when you press F9 to initiate a manual send/receive and/or if you want Outlook to still do a scheduled background send/receive (which may well involve initiating a dial-up connection to the Internet if that's how you connect).

▼▼▼▼▼

Caution: Geek Content Ahead!

Offline mode really only applies to Exchange server users, and it describes the condition where Outlook can't connect to the Exchange server. Outlook versions before 2003 could be configured to have an Offline Folder, which would synchronize periodically, typically when you closed Outlook, so that you could use Outlook in offline mode with a copy of the folder that was as current as the last sync you performed as you were signing off. This was mostly for laptop users who might be away from the office and unable to connect, at least at that time, to their Exchange server. Outlook 2003 and 2007 have "Cached Mode," which constantly caches the Exchange Mailbox to a local Offline Folders File (OST) so that when you're not able to connect to the Exchange server—either because your network is being slow or because you're on an airplane at 35,000 feet with no connectivity—you can still access Outlook and all of the items that are in your offline folder file as of the last time you were connected.

Mail Format Tab

The Mail Format tab lets you configure a number of options related to how your messages send. You'll notice if you were a user of previous versions of Outlook that Outlook no longer lets you select the Word Editor as your default mail editor. That's because the Word Editor is the *only* editor in Outlook 2007. There is no more Outlook Editor. What if you don't have Word installed? Never fear—Outlook comes with a stripped-down, purpose-built version of Word 2007 to use as its editor.

The Mail Format tab is also where you can configure your default message format (HTML by default) and where you can configure your e-mail signatures as we touched on in Chapter 2.

The Spelling Tab

The Spelling tab has only two options on it, and they're fairly self-explanatory. The first option is "Always check spelling before sending," which simply tells Outlook (or rather, Word, since that is the editor) to automatically run a spell check whenever the user clicks Send.

The other option on the Spelling tab is "Ignore original message text in reply or forward." That tells Word not to bother checking the spelling of text you're quoting. That's really just good manners—if the person who wrote to you misspelled something, you really don't need to correct it.

True Story

I once had the partners of a client firm come to me and insist that I turn on "Always check spelling before sending" for one of their partners; his spelling was so atrocious, they were concerned that it affected the perception of the clients with whom he corresponded.

The Other Tab

The Other tab is a catch-all for miscellaneous settings (Figure 9.34). Let's take a look at a couple of useful ones:

- **Empty the Deleted Items folder upon exiting:** This setting will automatically dump your Deleted Items folder whenever you exit Outlook. It's a handy way to make sure your Deleted Items folder stays clean and your mailbox stays relatively lean.
- **AutoArchive:** This tool helps you set your default AutoArchive settings.
- **Outlook Panes:** These buttons help you configure the behavior of Outlook's various Navigation, Reading, and To-Do Bar panes.

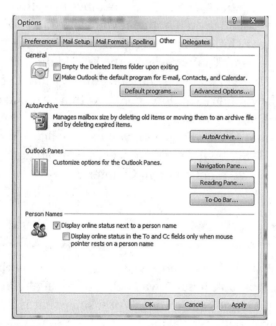

FIGURE 9.34

Backing Up Your Data

If you haven't backed it up, then you don't deserve to have it. If you have an Exchange server, then your IT person or consultant should have taken care of making sure your server is being regularly backed up, but that doesn't help you get your Personal Folders Files (PSTs) backed up if you don't have an Exchange server or if you have a local PST file in addition to your Exchange mailbox.

Backing up your PST files can be as simple as using the Windows Backup tool on your workstation to back up all of your personal data (look at Start | Programs | Accessories | System Tools. . .) or even just copying the PST file to a flash drive, CD/DVD, or another computer across a network.

▼

Make sure that if you do have an Exchange server backup that the backups being performed on it are "online backups." Online backups clean out the Exchange log files automatically. If that doesn't happen, the log files will build up and eventually fill up the server storage with unhappy results.

If you want a more sophisticated tool for backing up your PST files, Microsoft provides the PST Backup utility, which you can find here: http://office.microsoft.com/en-us/outlook/HA010875321033.aspx. It's free.

▼▼▼▼▼

Can't Open That PST from the CD?

If you stored a PST file on a CD or DVD and try to open it later, you may find that Outlook protests. Don't panic. Outlook requires read *and* write access to a PST file in order to open it. The odds are excellent that you only need to copy that PST file to a hard drive, right-click the file under Windows Explorer, and choose properties to make sure it's not Read-Only, and *then* you should be able to open it with Outlook.

AutoArchive

AutoArchive is a nifty way to help keep your mailbox lean by moving old messages off to a separate file. You can define how old is old—or even if archiving will run at all—on a folder-by-folder basis. AutoArchive can be configured to run automatically either with or without prompting you first.

To configure AutoArchive on an individual folder, right-click the folder in the folder list and choose Properties. Then click the AutoArchive tab in the properties dialog box (Figure 9.35).

There are three main options you can configure here:

- **Do not archive items in this folder:** Enough said?
- **Archive items in this folder using the default settings:** This will set this folder to play just like all the other folders. Click the "Default Archive Settings" button if you want to see what those settings are or make changes to them.

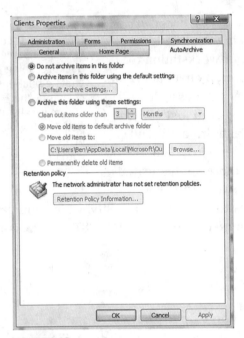

FIGURE 9.35

- **Archive this folder using these settings:** This is where things get interesting. You can specify how old items should be before AutoArchive acts upon them (the default is three months), and you can define what should be done with them. You have three choices of action here:

  - *Move old items to default archive folder:* Items will be moved, clearly enough, to the default archive folder for your profile—to where most of your folders are archived—it's probably a PST file called "archive.pst."

  - *Move old items to:* lets you define an alternate PST file to which you'd like to archive this folder. If you've got separate archive PST files for each client or case, then it might make sense to have this folder archive directly into the PST file for this client or case.

  - *Permanently delete old items:* I don't think I need to explain this one. Items permanently deleted will not appear in the Deleted Items folder.

Why Didn't My Items Archive?

A common question in the newsgroups is when somebody sets up AutoArchive and items that are apparently older than the threshold period fail to AutoArchive. What you need to understand is that AutoArchive looks at the *modified* date of the item—not the received or sent date. If you've recently moved the item to a new folder, then the modified date would be the date of that move, which could be quite recent.

Mailbox Cleanup

Most of you are going to have some kind of mailbox size quota, which will limit how large your mailbox can get. Even if you don't, however, there is a definite advantage to keeping your mailbox relatively lean: it will perform better, be more stable, and be more usable. Outlook 2007 provides a handy "Mailbox Cleanup" tool, which you can find on the Tools menu.

Emptying Deleted Items

The Deleted Items folder is one area where lots of waste can occur. Emptying it is as simple as can be; in fact, there are at least three simple ways to do so. One is to simply right-click the Deleted Items folder and select "Empty Deleted Items" from the context menu.

Emptying Junk E-mail

Junk E-mail is another folder that should get emptied out regularly. Unlike Deleted Items, you probably didn't put most of these items in this folder, so it is sometimes worth a quick scan of the folder to make sure there aren't any legitimate messages in here that actually shouldn't have been flagged as spam. Once you're confident that all of the messages in this folder are, in fact, spam, you can go ahead and empty it by right-clicking the folder name and choosing "Empty Junk E-mail" from the Context menu that appears.

Summary

Outlook is a powerful program, and there are a lot of configuration settings that can help you configure how Outlook operates. With some careful tweaking you can control message format, the default location where items are stored, how the indexing will work, and even if your Outlook trash gets dumped at the end of every workday. For that matter you can even tell Outlook when the end (and beginning) of your workday *is!*

Troubleshooting 10

When things go wrong, as they sometimes do, it can be very helpful to understand how to diagnose the problem and resolve it if necessary.

Nondelivery Reports (NDRs)

Occasionally, when you send an e-mail message, you may get a message back that says something like:

> Your message did not reach some or all of the intended recipients.
>
> Subject: Baker Settlement
> Sent: 12/11/2006 11:19 AM
>
> The following recipient(s) could not be reached:
>
> smab@boguslawfirm.com on 12/11/2006 11:19 AM
> The e-mail account does not exist at the organization this message was sent to. Check the e-mail address, or contact the recipient directly to find out the correct address.
> <server.myfirm.com #5.1.1>

Translating these messages to figure out what went wrong can be a somewhat difficult process for an end user, but I'll spend a page or three here to help you decipher them a bit so that you can have a good talk with your IT people about what might have happened. The first thing you need to understand is that the content of NDR messages is not standardized and can vary a bit from server to server. Some will be fairly clear, and some will be quite esoteric.

The first thing to look at is the explanatory text, if there is any. In our sample NDR above, the explanatory text is actually quite revealing. It says rather clearly that the e-mail account does not exist at the organization to which the message was sent. Generally speaking, that means that the address is probably wrong—though it could also mean that the user no longer exists, so if you're sure the address is correct, it's possible that the person you're writing to no longer works there—and in this case I can see one obvious possibility for the address to be wrong. The username "smab" seems a little odd. Could it possibly be "SamB"?

Other common examples of useful explanatory text might be that the recipient's mailbox is over quota, which means it's too full and can't accept your message right now; the message you're trying to send exceeds their maximum message limit, which means that you need to find some way to reduce the size of your message—most likely your message is too large due to one or more attachments; or your message has possibly been rejected by their spam filter—in which case you may need to consult with their mail administrator to see how you can resolve that issue.

If the explanatory text is not useful, the next thing to look at is the three-digit code toward the end of the message. If the code begins with a 4 (such as #4.2.2), that generally means a temporary condition has stymied your message delivery. Some examples of that could be that the recipient's mailbox is full, her server is out of disk space, her server is not accepting e-mail messages at the moment, or some other similar issue. If the code begins with a 5 (such as #5.2.3), then the problem is usually more permanent. For example, #5.1.2 usually means that the domain name couldn't be resolved, which usually means that it has been mistyped in the e-mail message.

A Few Common NDR Codes	
The Code	**What It Means**
4.2.2	The recipient's mailbox is over its limit.
4.3.1	Not enough disk space on the delivery server.
5.1.1	Recipient address doesn't exist.
5.1.2	Host name can't be found. Probably means you mistyped the domain name.
5.2.x	Any 5.2.x error code will typically mean that the message is too large. Probably due to one or more big attachments.
5.3.1	Tends to mean the recipient's mail system is full.

Profiles

Each Outlook user has a profile that contains the customizations they've made to Outlook, the e-mail accounts they use, and other settings unique to that user. Sometimes Outlook profiles can get corrupted, in which case the easiest solution is usually to create a new one.

To create a new profile, go to Control Panel and open the Mail applet. The result is the "Mail Setup – Outlook" dialog you can see in Figure 10.1. Click the "Show Profiles" button, and you'll get the "Mail" dialog box in Figure 10.2.

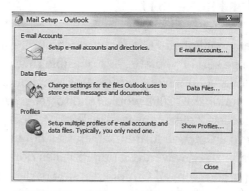

FIGURE 10.1

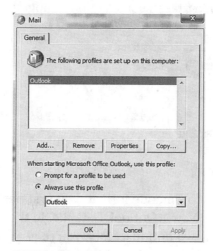

FIGURE 10.2

If for some reason you can't find the Mail applet, you may have to start it manually. To do so, go to the C:\Program Files\Microsoft Office\ Office12 folder, and look for MLCFG32.CPL. Occasionally, especially on Vista systems, the Mail applet won't appear in Control Panel.

Once you've started the Mail Applet, click the Show Profiles button to get the dialog box you see in Figure 10.2. From here you can easily add a new profile by clicking the "Add" button, which will step you through the process of creating the profile, configuring the mail accounts, and specifying the default data store(s). Before you finish with this dialog box, you should check the "Prompt for a profile to be used" radio button if you're creating a second profile for testing. Next time you start Outlook it will ask you which profile you want to start with—that makes it easy for you to test (or use) multiple profiles within the same Windows user account.

Personal Folder Files (PST)

If you're using a Personal Folders File for storing your items—and unless you have an Exchange server you are—it's possible that your file has gotten corrupted. In older versions of Outlook, this was not an unusual condition; PST files in Outlook 97–2002 would tend to get corrupted as they approached or exceeded 2 gigabytes in size. With Outlook 2003, Microsoft upgraded PST files to a Unicode format, which was not susceptible to the same file size limitations. However, existing PST files don't get automatically upgraded. If you upgrade from an Outlook version earlier than 2003 (or if you upgraded to 2003 from an earlier version), your PST file will still be in the old format if you haven't taken some action to upgrade it (Figure 10.3).

FIGURE 10.3

Upgrading Your PST

To upgrade your PST file to Unicode format, you first need to create a new PST file by going to File | New | Outlook Data file. In the New Outlook Data File dialog box, you'll get two options. Since you're not going to be sharing this data file with an older version of Outlook, you'll want to create an "Office Outlook Personal Folders File," which is a Unicode file—far more robust and stable than the old style (Figure 10.4). Not surprisingly, it's not backwards compatible—Outlook 2000, for instance, cannot read a Unicode PST file. If you really need to share the PST file between the versions, you'll need to create an "Outlook 97–2002 Personal Folders File." Bear in mind, however, that the Outlook 97–2002 Personal Folders File is going to suffer from the same limitations and issues as did the original files. Just because it was created and/or used by Outlook 2003 or 2007 doesn't fix the considerable issues that format of PST file had—especially the corruption issues.

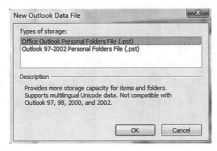

FIGURE 10.4

After you select the file type you want and click OK, you'll get a dialog box that asks you to name the PST file and select a location to store it. This is a Windows filename (i.e., the name you'll see if you look at the directory with Windows Explorer). After you give the PST file a name and click OK, you'll get the "Create Microsoft Personal Folders" dialog box, which asks you to give your PST file a name (this is a name for Outlook to display, not a Windows filename) (Figure 10.5). It's best to change the name from the default of "Personal Folders" to something else like "Primary Data File" or "My New Data File" to make it easier to discern when you have both files open in Outlook.

FIGURE 10.5

Once you've created your new PST file, you should see both files in the Folder List of Outlook 2007. Now for the painful part—you don't want to use File I Import and Export to move your existing items to your new PST file. That sometimes causes problems with dates in Outlook. Instead, you want to drag and drop items from one folder to the other. It's not quite as bad as it sounds. For the primary folders like Inbox, Sent Items, or Contacts, just open the folder in your old file, select any item, press CTRL+A to select all, then drag and drop the whole lot of them to the same folder in the new file. To move your calendar items, first change the view to "All Appointments" then select any item and press CTRL+A to select all and drag. If you're having trouble dragging and dropping the items, just right-click the folder or items and select "Move to Folder," which will help you move them.

To move subfolders to your new PST, just drag each folder from your old PST file to the same location in your new PST file. You don't have to drag the individual items in those. Yes, it's a little irritating, but you should only have to do it once, and once it's done, it's done.

ScanPST

If your PST file does become corrupted, there is a tool included with Outlook that can check for errors and fix them if possible. That tool is called "SCANPST.EXE" and you'll generally find it in C:\Program Files\Microsoft Office (Figure 10.6). Run that tool, point it to the PST file you're having problems with, and let it scan the file. This can take several minutes, but when it's done, hopefully your file will be repaired. If not, give ScanPST another chance; sometimes it takes multiple passes for the problems to be completely fixed. I will generally keep running ScanPST until it says there are no more errors found (or until I decide the PST file is beyond repair because ScanPST had taken a lot of passes at it without completely fixing the issue).

FIGURE 10.6

Corrupted OST Files

If you have an Exchange server and you are running Outlook in Cached Mode (and you should), then you will have an OST file for your profile. The OST file is an Offline Folder File, which is where Outlook stores its cached local version of the mailbox. Like the PST file, it's possible for the OST file to occasionally get corrupted, and there actually *is* a ScanOST program on your machine that operates just like the ScanPST program; however, unless there is data in your OST file that has not been synchronized to your Exchange mailbox, there isn't any point in fixing it. Just delete the OST file, and the next time you start Outlook and connect to your Exchange server, Outlook will automatically recreate the OST file for you.

Detect and Repair

If Outlook won't start or if it's having other problems that you can't seem to resolve, try doing a Detect and Repair; it's a fairly harmless option that won't touch your data. To initiate it, go to Control Panel | Add/Remove Programs, or in Vista go to "Programs and Features." Find Microsoft Office 2007 and select Change. You'll get a dialog box that includes "Repair" as an option (Figure 10.7). Select "Repair" and click "Continue." Let it run the repair—it'll check all of Outlook's program files and settings and fix any that seem to be broken. Sometimes it fixes the problem, and it rarely creates any new problems—a fairly painless thing to try—unlike our next technique. . . .

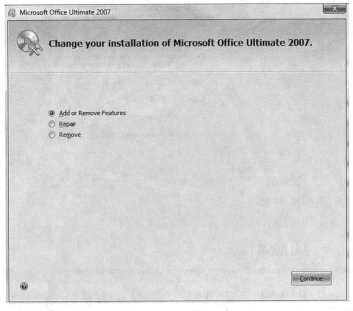

FIGURE 10.7

System Restore

This one you should check out with your IT staff or consultants (if you have any) before you try it. Windows XP and Vista both have a System Restore capability that can restore your system back to the condition it was in at a previous date (Figure 10.8). You'll find System Restore under Start | Programs | All Programs | Accessories | System Tools. System Restore doesn't affect any of your data or documents; instead, it restores your settings and system files back to the condition they were in on the selected date. Ideally, you would pick a date when you know the system was working fine and let System Restore try to put the computer back into that condition. If you've installed any new software or changed any settings since then, that software/settings will likely be lost and will have to be reinstalled or reconfigured. Like I said, check with your IT guys or gals before you do this. However, it is generally possible to un-restore if the restored condition proves unacceptable. This is a more drastic step than Detect and Repair, however, so proceed with care.

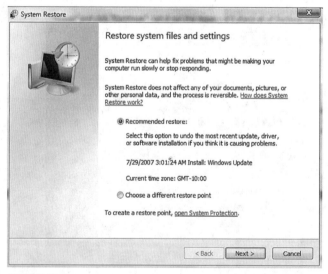

FIGURE 10.8

Outlook Safe Mode

Outlook can tend to accumulate a lot of add-ins and extensions to do various things like allow iTunes to synchronize your calendar to your iPod. If Outlook is slow or unstable, you might try starting it in Safe Mode—which disables all of the add-ins and extensions—to see if the problem goes away. To start Outlook 2007 in Safe Mode just press and hold the CTRL key when you start Outlook. To get out of Safe Mode, just close Outlook and restart it normally.

Getting Help

If you have a problem or question I haven't answered here, there are lots of resources available for you to get more help with Outlook 2007.

Help

If you bought any software back in the early '90s, you probably remember when software used to come with a big printed manual. Not anymore—the manuals were expensive to write and print and added considerably to the packaging costs. And, frankly, very few people read them anyhow. So today the content that used to go into the printed manual now goes into the help file. To get to the help system in Outlook, just look to the right-hand end of the menu bar for the Help Search field (Figure 10.9). Outlook 2007 integrates help files on your computer with online help. This has the benefit that Microsoft can continually add to and update the help system, and you will always have the latest copy available.

FIGURE 10.9

How to Call Support

If you ever have to call technical support, there are a few basics that you need to be ready to provide to make the experience as smooth and easy as possible.

- What operating system (OS) you're using. Windows XP? Vista? Home? Pro? Ultimate?
- Do you have all of the service packs installed?
- What version of the product are you using? Outlook 2007?
- What exactly are you trying to do?
- What, if any, error messages are you getting?
- Are you the only one having the problem, or is it occurring for others in your firm as well?
- When did the problem start? Do you know of anything in your computer that changed just before that?
- What, if anything, have you already tried to do to fix it?

Microsoft Technical Communities

The same guidelines for calling support also extend to asking for help by e-mail or in the Microsoft Technical Communities, or "newsgroups." Some folks don't realize that Microsoft provides free newsgroups or forums where you can post questions and see the answers others have posted.

> **MVPs**
>
> MVPs are Microsoft's Most Valuable Professionals. They are a group of volunteers who have been recognized by Microsoft for their contributions in their product communities. Nearly every Microsoft product has MVPs. You'll commonly find them in the newsgroups.

There are one or more newsgroups for every product that Microsoft makes (yes, including Xbox) as well as newsgroups in a dozen different languages. There are two basic ways to access them:

Web Interface

To access the forums through the Web Interface go to http://www.microsoft .com/communities/newsgroups/ default.mspx and find the newsgroups that interest you. By following the links for the product or area that you're interested in, you'll eventually be led to the forum where you can post or read questions or answers about that product.

NNTP (Network News Transfer Protocol)

The "classic" way to access the newsgroups is by using an NNTP reader such as Outlook Express (OE) or Vista's "Windows Mail." That's how most of the "power users" (like me) access the newsgroups. In Windows Mail it's quite easy because Vista comes with the Microsoft Technical Communities predefined. You just click on it, and it gives you a list of the newsgroups to which you can choose to subscribe. Yes, they're free. Subscribe to as many or as few newsgroups as you want to, and click on them to read the messages posted or post your own (Figure 10.10).

Follow these steps to use Outlook Express (or any other news reader) to read the Microsoft newsgroups:

1. In Outlook Express click "Tools."
2. Select "Accounts."
3. Click the "News" tab.
4. Click the "Add" button and select "News."
5. In the ensuing wizard, type a Display Name. This is how you'll appear to folks who see your posts—you can use your real name or an alias. Generally, it's good to type some variation of your real name, even if just your first name. Click Next.

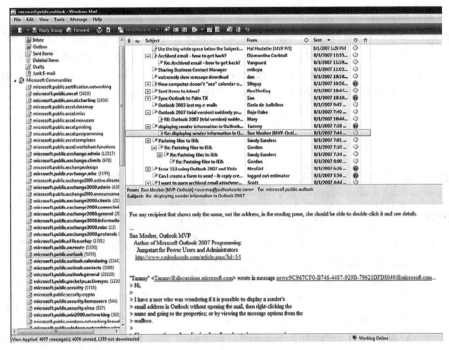

FIGURE 10.10

6. Outlook Express will then ask you for your e-mail address.
    CAUTION: I strongly advise against putting your real e-mail
    address here. Spammers harvest addresses from the news-
    groups, so putting your real address here is an open invitation
    for an influx of spam. You can put a bogus address here with
    no problem—I use bens@bogusaddress.mvp myself. You could
    use yourname@yourfirm.law if you wanted to. If you really need
    to put a real address here because you want folks to reply to
    you, I'd suggest you get a Hotmail or Gmail account—you don't
    care if those get blasted by spam. Click Next.

7. The wizard will ask you for the name of the news server. Type
    msnews.microsoft.com. No password is required.

8. Click Next until you can click "Finish," and OE will offer to download
    the list of newsgroups for you. There are thousands of them.

That's all you need to do. The newsgroups can be a wealth of free
information and advice—just remember that the other folks who are there
answering questions are primarily volunteers doing that in their spare time.
You may get an answer to your question in minutes, or it may take days, or,
in rare cases, you might not get an answer. Most of the time you'll get one
or more very good answers, but just remember what you paid for it.

Google Groups

Google Groups is a handy way to search the newsgroups, both Microsoft's and others. Just go to http://groups.google.com. It's the familiar Google search interface, and you can search (for free) all of the newsgroups. You will often find that your question has already been asked and answered right there. Don't panic. Do look for help.

Popular Web Resources

There are a few Web sites worth knowing about for Outlook 2007.

- **Microsoft.com/outlook:** rather obviously the official site for Microsoft Outlook 2007.
- **Slipstick.com:** Funny name, but for years has been one of the best resources for Outlook information. Run by Outlook MVP Diane Poremsky.
- **OfficeForLawyers.com:** Shameless plug alert! A site developed by me, to host information related to Microsoft Office for lawyers and to support this book and the others in the series.
- **Outlook-tips.com:** another good site of Outlook information; includes free Outlook tips e-mailed to you (or delivered via RSS) three times a week.

Sync Issues

The Sync Issues folder, which you can find by going to the Folder List, is a local folder in your Offline Folder File (OST). It is only of use to you if you have an Exchange server and contains messages that occur when Outlook has trouble synchronizing content in some manner with the Exchange server. There can be a variety of reasons for synchronization errors and conflicts, some of them harmless, others not so much. There are three subfolders of Sync Issues. Let's take a quick look at the basic items you'll find in these folders.

Synchronization Logs

These log files can help you to see what may be wrong with your synchronization but in most cases are only going to be useful for your IT staff or consultants. Outlook will generate one each time something doesn't go quite right with your synchronization. This is not always a serious issue, but your IT staff or consultant should be able to look at the log and tell you.

Conflicts

The Conflicts folder contains items where there are different changes made to different copies of the item. This sounds a little complicated but essentially it usually happens when you have more than one device synchronizing the same folder—for example, I sometimes have both the computer on my desk AND my Tablet PC connected to my Exchange mailbox at the same time and both of them are synchronizing at roughly the same time. Because these syncs don't always happen at exactly the same moment and because I may be using one, or both, machines and making changes to items, if my changes happen to occur at an inopportune moment in the synchronization process, the result could be conflicting copies of items. At the top of the conflicted message you'll find an infobar that will give you the opportunity to merge the changes between the conflicted items.

Local Failures

The Local Failures folder contains items where Outlook was unable to successfully send the items to the server—items you created locally but that couldn't sync to the server for some reason.

Server Failures

This is the converse of the Local Failures folder—items that are on the server but that failed to sync down to the local OST file.

Persistent synchronization issues are indicative of potentially more serious problems. The only easy "fix" you can try as an end user is to rename or delete your OST file in case the problem is corruption in the OST file. You'll only want to try that while you're connected to the Exchange server so that Outlook can readily rebuild the OST file. Be wary of renaming or deleting the OST file if you have unsynchronized items that you care about in your local store, such as appointments or e-mails that you created in Outlook but that have not yet synchronized to the server. In that case, renaming or deleting the OST file should be considered a last resort. If you're otherwise current, though, then there's no harm in letting Outlook create a new OST file except that it may take a little while to complete and while it rebuilds, the OST file performance may not be great.

If renaming or deleting the OST file doesn't resolve the synchronization issues then you'll have to get your IT staff or consultants involved, as the problem is something somewhat more complicated and esoteric.

Summary

When things go wrong, as they sometimes do, there are things you can do to help Outlook get back on track. Creating a new profile or starting Outlook in safe mode are two pretty common solutions, but lots more, and lots of less common, solutions can be found by accessing the wealth of troubleshooting resources for Outlook.

Mistakes Lawyers Make with Outlook 11

Over the last decade I've had plenty of chances to observe lawyers in action with Outlook, and I've been able to shake my head and chuckle at the mistakes they've made with it. Let's spend this time together talking about those mistakes so you can stop making them. Remember, I'm not laughing at you, I'm laughing toward you.

Deleted Items Storage

"You have 21,453 items in your deleted items folder," I observed. "Why don't you empty that out?" "Oh, no! I can't empty it—there might be important things in there!" replied the attorney.

If I had a nickel for every time a lawyer has told me they can't empty their Deleted Items folder because there are, or might be, important things in it, I would have a lot of nickels. You don't store important client documents in your trash can, do you? Then don't store important e-mails or other items in your Deleted Items folder.

▼

If you have an Exchange server, ask your Exchange administrator to enable "Deleted Item Retention" so that in the event you do accidentally delete and then subsequently purge an important item, you can still recover it. Be careful though, if delete doesn't really mean delete, that can have implications in eDiscovery.

The Deleted Items folder is the Outlook equivalent of your trash can. It's a place where stuff goes that you want to toss out, and until the cleaning crew comes along and dumps it, you could still reach in there and pluck back the document that inadvertently fell in. Just like your trash can, it's important that your Deleted Items folder gets emptied out from time to time. Otherwise, items in there consume valuable space in your message store.

To empty the Deleted Items folder, just click Tools | Empty Deleted Items folder.

Misaddressing Messages

One of the advantages of e-mail is how easy it is to just address something and click "Send." You can send to individual e-mail accounts within your firm, to distribution lists, or to e-mail accounts out in the world all with just a few clicks. However, this ease of use means that users can very easily misaddress a message and send that message somewhere it was never intended to go.

You want to send an e-mail to your associate Judy Lawrence about tactics for petitioning for a change of venue because you think Judge Tucker will be unsympathetic to your client. You enter your message, type "Jud" in the To field, and accept the first AutoSuggested address. You click Send just a split second before you realize that the address Outlook has AutoSuggested was judgetucker@courts.gov.

The lesson here is to very carefully check your addressing before you send.

Tasks on the Calendar

In previous versions of Outlook, the Tasks folder was only accessible as a separate folder or as a Tasks Pane alongside the Calendar. However, the days on the Task Pane didn't necessarily relate to the Calendar days displayed. Users wanted to be able to look at a date on the Calendar and see all of their appointments *and* tasks due on that date in a single, easy interface.

Their solution was to add tasks to the Calendar, frequently as "All Day Appointments." Unfortunately, that's not really how the Calendar is intended to be used. If your task has a particular date/time element to it, such as "Call Judge at 10:00 a.m. on Friday," then it makes sense to schedule it as an appointment. If it's just a To-Do item with a due date (but not time) such as "forward accident scene photos to insurance adjuster," then it makes more sense to keep it as a "Task" instead of an appointment.

With Outlook 2007, Microsoft has placed the tasks on their own bar underneath the calendar called the "Daily Task List." This should alleviate the issue of not seeing the tasks on the same day as the appointments and hopefully will steer people back to using Tasks as intended.

Many Are the Outlook Windows

Every time you double-click an item it opens a new inspector window. If you don't close that item—or Outlook doesn't—when you're done with it, those inspector windows will tend to accumulate. The more common thing I see, however, is lawyers who repeatedly open Outlook instances because they have minimized it or opened other applications over it and don't realize that it's still running.

There is a time and place for multiple Outlook windows, but too often they get away from the user. Be aware of how many Outlook windows are running (you can see them on the Task bar), and close any that aren't in use. Every open window consumes resources. If you don't see Outlook on the screen, check the Task bar to see if it's open but minimized, or look for the Outlook icon on the system tray.

Remember that if you start Outlook from the Quick Launch bar (next to the Start button, typically), you launch a new instance of Outlook.

Printing E-mail

This is a mistake I usually see older lawyers make. These lawyers are more comfortable working with paper and don't feel that electronic records are viable. While it's perfectly OK to print the occasional e-mail, I sometimes see

Recycling Is Good

Recycling is good not only for the Earth but also for your resource usage. If you right-click the Quick Launch shortcut you use to start Outlook and choose "Properties," you should see the "Target" field, which shows what the shortcut is pointing to. If it isn't already there, add the "/recycle" (without the quotes) switch to the end of the line so that if Outlook is already open, the shortcut won't open a new instance.

lawyers who insist upon printing and filing every e-mail they receive. This is a needless waste of paper and storage space.

Instead, store your e-mails in folders, print only key messages, and archive those e-mails into .PST files, which you can burn onto CDs to include with the client or matter file.

Where's My Toolbar?

Right-click on the toolbar or menu bar in Outlook. You'll get a context menu you may not remember seeing before (Figure 11.1). This context menu lets you turn on or off the toolbars. It's easy for folks who are awkward with the mouse to try and left-click on a menu bar or toolbar button but "fat finger" the mouse and accidentally click the right button at the same time. The context menu appears and they unintentionally left-click on it, un-checking one or more of the toolbars in the process. I've seen it happen lots of times.

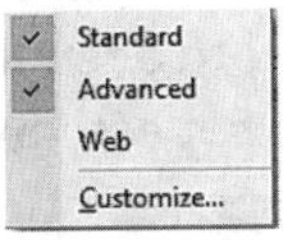

FIGURE 11.1

The remedy is simple: right-click that toolbar again and re-check the missing bar(s).

Where Are My Messages?

Views are great things that can help you see just the items you want in just the way you want. If you're not careful though, they can also hide things you want. From time to time, I get a call from a user who says, "Hey, all of my messages older than last week are gone!" or "Every time I open and read a message, when I go back to my Inbox it's been deleted!" While it's possible that the user is accidentally deleting those messages, it's more likely they have inadvertently turned on a view of their Inbox that is hiding their messages.

The "Last Seven Days" view is going to hide all e-mail older than the last week, while the "Unread Mail" view is going to hide messages that have been marked as read. The messages are still there, they've just been hidden.

Change your view back to "Messages," and you should see everything.

Summary

I see people make several common mistakes with Outlook. Most of them involve the storage and viewing of items, and most of them can be avoided with just a little careful thought. Avoiding these mistakes can help keep you more productive.

Tricks to Impress Your Law School Classmates **12**

Outlook is the application the majority of Office users use most, but nearly all of them use only a small bit of its features. It's also the application where most users *love* to learn new tricks. Here are a few that will make your friends smile.

> Any sufficiently advanced technology is indistinguishable from magic.
>
> —*Arthur C. Clarke*

Natural Language Dates

The practice of law is often about figuring our relative dates: "What's ninety days after next Tuesday?" for instance. Some court reporters and other support companies have even had "Date Calculator" wheels printed up (with their logos all over them, of course) for lawyers, paralegals, and legal secretaries to use to figure such things out. Fortunately, Outlook stands ready for the task. Need to create a task item to call a client tomorrow? Start your new task item, and in the Due Date field, type "tomorrow." Click on or tab to another field, and watch what the Due Date field does.

Need to submit your time sheets on Friday? Start the new task item, and in the Due Date field type "Friday." Click on or tab to another field, and watch what the Due Date field does.

Having lunch with Judge Eddy next Tuesday? Start your new appointment item, click on the Date field and type "next Tuesday." Guess what the Due Date field will do.

▼

Do you really need to type the "+" symbol to add the days, weeks, or months as specified? No, not really, but it does make for an intuitive delimiter, so I encourage it just to make it a little more natural. If you resent the extra keystroke and are comfortable with the awkward syntax, you can just type "tomorrow2d," and it will work just as well.

It gets better. Need to file a brief sixty days from Wednesday? Start your new task item, click in the Due Date field, and type "Wed +60d." Yes, Outlook will calculate that date for you.

There are all sorts of permutations you can try. Outlook recognizes "week" and "month," too. Play with it, and you'll find some very useful little tricks.

Customized Views

Some folks want to create separate folders to organize items and keep them separate. Unfortunately, your folder tree can get quickly out of control and become unwieldy. It's much better to use custom views to sort and filter the items in a folder in a more useful way. One of the best examples of this would be the Contacts folder. Rather than creating a separate Contacts folder for the members of your Homeowners Association, just create a category for them and create a custom view that filters on that category. Let's take a look at how you can do that:

1. Create a new Contact item—enter the name and whatever other information you want.
2. Before you save and close, click the "Categorize" button on the ribbon, and select "All Categories." The "Color Categories" dialog box similar to what you see in Figure 12.1 will appear.

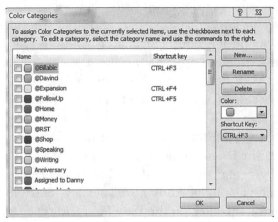

FIGURE 12.1

3. Click the "New" button to create a new category. Name it whatever works for you. Let me teach you a quick trick for forcing a category to the top of the list: Preface it with a symbol like "@" or a number (symbols come before numbers on the list). Select a color to represent that category, and if you think you'll use that category a lot and want to have a keyboard shortcut to assign it, you can select it here as well. Click OK to save it.

4. Check the box in front of the category you want to assign that contact to. Yes, you can assign as many categories as you like—in case this contact is a member of the Homeowners Association *and* your tennis club as well.

5. Save and close the contact item.

That's the first part. Next we need to create the custom view with the filter.

1. Click View | Current View | Define Views. The Current View Organizer will appear as in Figure 12.2.

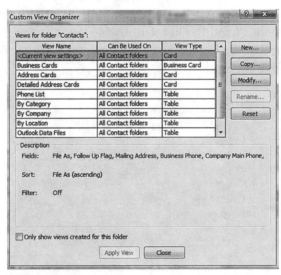

FIGURE 12.2

2. It's probably easier to just base your new view off an existing view, so pick a view you like—Address Cards is a favorite of mine—and copy it by selecting it and clicking Copy.

3. Give your new view a name that makes sense to you, "Homeowners Association" for instance, and decide where you want this view to apply (Figure 12.3). To be honest, the "Can be used on" setting is not all that important. It only determines if the new entry will be available in other folders and if anybody else will

be able to view it. Since this is your personal Contacts folder we're looking at, it probably doesn't much matter if you change this setting.

FIGURE 12.3

4. When you click "OK," the Customize View dialog will appear. The only setting we need to change here is to set the filter by clicking the "Filter" button.

5. When the Filter dialog box appears, click the "More Choices" tab (Figure 12.4). You could type the name of your category in the Categories field, but it's better to just click the Categories button and select it from the list. Otherwise you run the risk of mistyping the name of the category, and if you don't get it exactly right, the filter isn't going to work.

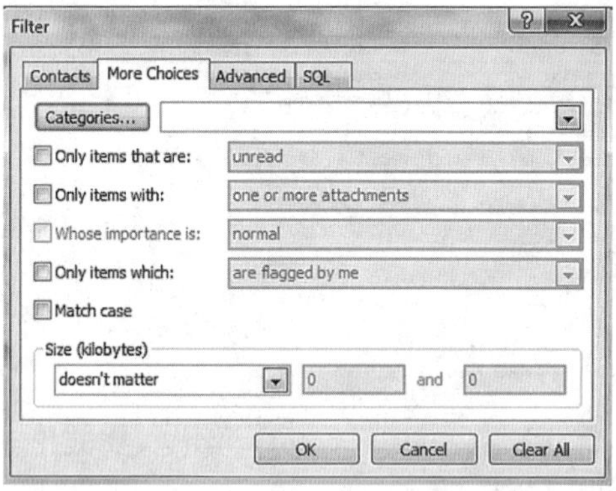

FIGURE 12.4

6. Click OK all the way back to the Custom View Organizer, then click Apply View to turn your fancy new view on and admire the results.

You can use this technique to create as many views as you like.

If you just want to create a quick filtered view that you're not necessarily going to use all the time, you can modify the current view to turn the filter on or off. Click View | Current View | Customize Current View, and adjust the filter settings just like we did above. Or right-click on or under the alphabetical tabs at the right side of the Explorer window, and select "Filter" from the context menu that appears.

Later, when you want to turn the filter back off, just go back into the Filter settings and click the "Clear All" button, then OK your way back out.

Open in a New Window

Sometimes you'll be working in your Inbox and want to see your Calendar too. You may get a little frustrated switching back and forth and think it would be really handy to be able to open them both at the same time. Luckily . . . you can. Open the Mail group, and right-click the Calendar group on the Navigation Pane (Figure 12.5). The first option on the resulting context menu is "Open in New Window," which, as you might guess, will open the selected folder in a new window so that you can see them both at the same time. This is especially effective in a dual-monitor environment but will work fine with just one monitor too. I have three other things to say about this:

FIGURE 12.5

1. Will it work on other folders too? Yes, any folder. Even other mail folders, in case you want to see two mail folders side by side.
2. Can I open more than two windows at once? Yes, as many as your system is capable of (the limiting factor will probably be memory). Of course, you probably won't have enough screen space to usefully view more than a handful of windows at once anyhow.
3. Relating to #2 . . . don't get crazy. Every Outlook window you open takes resources from your system, and there is a limit to how many windows you can see on the screen at the same time anyhow.

Delayed Delivery

It's Sunday afternoon, and you've just remembered that you want to send a client an e-mail on Tuesday reminding them to sign and return their

Tip

Worried about accidentally sending the message before you've set the "Delay Delivery" flag? Here's what I do: don't type anything in the To field until you're ready to send. That way you can be sure to add any attachments, make sure to proofread, set any options you want, and if you accidentally hit "Send" prematurely, the message won't go anywhere.

closing documents. You could create a task item for that but then it's another task you have to do on Tuesday and you're thinking about it now. Don't you wish you could just write the message now, but it wouldn't actually get sent to the client until later? Wish granted. Go ahead and start composing your new e-mail message, but before you click Send, go to the Options tab in the new message inspector and click the "Delay Delivery" button on the ribbon (Figure 12.6). This will open the message options dialog box that you can see in Figure 12.7, and under Delivery Options you'll find "Do not deliver before:"

FIGURE 12.6

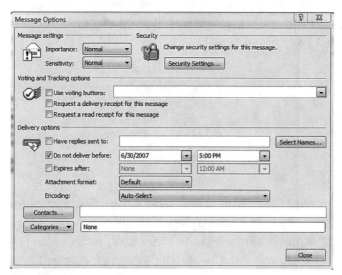

FIGURE 12.7

When you click "Send" on your message, it will stay in your Outbox until the designated date and time. There are two things I need to say about this feature before we move on.

1. The one danger of this technique is if you schedule a message to go out later in the week, something could happen before the message goes out that makes the message irrelevant or incorrect. Be aware of what's sitting in your Outbox. It would be embarrassing if the case settled on Monday, and you sent your client a delayed offer on Wednesday. This is not quite a "set it and forget it" feature.

2. When you exit Outlook, it's going to tell you that there are unsent messages in your Outbox. Just acknowledge it and exit.

I use this trick not only for messages to clients but also to send scheduled messages to folks when I know that I might not be available to send them in person. I once used it to send a "happy birthday" message to a friend when I knew that I'd be spending most of her birthday on airplanes and might not have a chance to send an e-mail or call her that day.

Clean Out the AutoComplete

When you compose a new e-mail message and start to type an e-mail address, Outlook will pop a window that suggests addresses you've used before. That's fine as long as the addresses are current and correct. But what happens when a wrong or old address gets into that list? Here's how you can clean the AutoComplete list out.

Clean House

Let's start with the scenario where you want to wipe the whole list clean and start over. The AutoComplete list is stored in a nickname file (with a .NK2 extension). The file is located in a hidden folder, the location of which will vary slightly depending upon if you're running Windows XP or Vista. Typically under Windows XP, you'll find it under C:\Documents and Settings\ [username]\Application Data\Microsoft\Outlook\[profile name].NK2. In Vista, you'll probably find it under C:\Users\[username]\AppData\Roaming\ Microsoft\[profile name].NK2. If you want to wipe out the AutoComplete list, just close Outlook and then delete that .NK2 file. Outlook will create a new, empty nickname file for you automatically the next time you open it.

One by One

Maybe you just want to delete one or two individual entries from the list without wiping the whole thing clean. In that case just start a new e-mail message in Outlook, click in the To field, and start typing the first few letters of the address you want to remove. When the AutoComplete window pops up, use your arrow keys (*not* your mouse!) to select the address you want to delete, and then just press the delete key. Simple as that.

Hide When Minimized

Outlook is a fairly robust program and uses quite a few system resources when it's open. One trick you can use to reduce the impact on your

▼

The nickname file will save the most recently used 1,000 addresses. As you add more addresses the least used ones are replaced. In previous versions of Outlook the nickname file was a little fragile and tended to corrupt when it got full. The consequences of that aren't especially severe, Outlook will simply replace the corrupted file with a new, empty one automatically.

system when you aren't using Outlook is to right-click the system tray icon and choose "Hide When Minimized" (Figure 12.8). Normally when you minimize Outlook, it will simply shrink to your Task bar as an item there. If you select "Hide When Minimized" and you minimize Outlook, it will disappear from the Task bar and only appear on the system tray. Not only does it get Outlook off the Task bar, leaving you a cleaner look, but it also slightly reduces Outlook's resource utilization on your machine.

FIGURE 12.8

Folder Home Pages

Outlook has the ability to display Web sites in the folder pane, and that's what Folder Home Pages are all about (Figure 12.9). There are some really powerful things that you can do with this feature, but those details are a tad beyond the scope of this book. For now, let me just say that if you right-click a folder and choose "Properties," then click the "Home Page" tab, you can type in the URL of a Web page (either on the Internet or on your internal network). Click the box for "Show home page by default for this folder"—you might as well, since there is no way in

Tip

Create a new folder specifically to be the link to this Web site rather than using an existing folder. When "Show folder home page by default for this folder" is checked, you won't be able to easily access the items in the folder, if there are any. That's why I just create purpose-built folders to do this with on those occasions when I want a folder home page in Outlook.

Outlook 2007 to turn the Folder Home Page on or off. Then whenever you click on that folder, Outlook will open the URL you've specified in the folder pane as you can see in Figure 12.10.

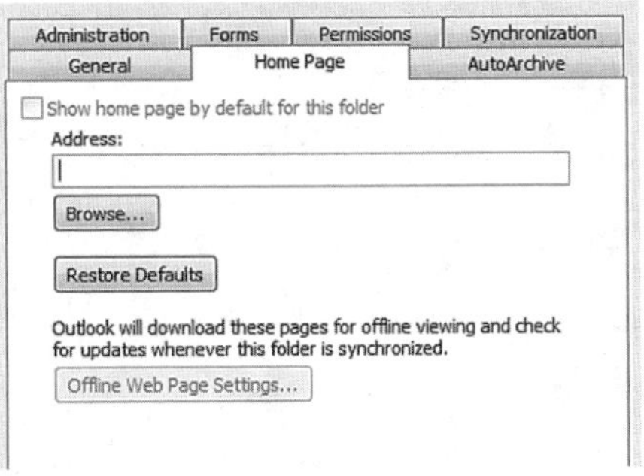

FIGURE 12.9

FIGURE 12.10

Find Items in Any Folder

It may be handy on occasion—for example, if you diligently use Categories to label items as relating to a particular case, client, or matter—to be able to search across all folders for items of different types in a single search.

To do this, use the Advanced Find tool by clicking Tools | Instant Search | Advanced Find, or press CTRL+SHIFT+F (Figure 12.11). Click the "Look for" field, and select "Any type of Outlook item." The "In" field, which dictates the scope of the search, will default to the entire default information store (either your mailbox or personal folders file, depending upon your configuration).

Once you've selected the item types and scope, you can set the criteria for your search. For instance, if you wanted to search by Category, you

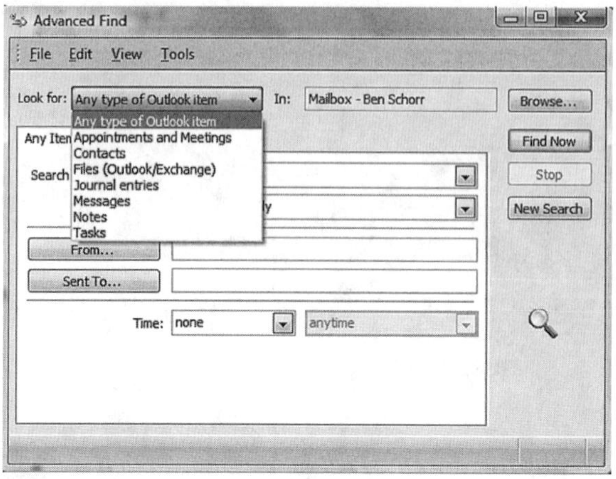

FIGURE 12.11

would click the More Choices tab where you can specify the Category or Categories that you want to search for (Figure 12.12).

The results are presented beneath the search box. I have to say that one area I hope the next version of Outlook improves upon is in the presentation of these results. As you can see in Figure 12.13, the results presented are a simple list that is not as easy to work with as most of the other Outlook search results. Double-click any item on the list in order to open, view, and/or edit the item.

Be aware that the "All Items" search is also going to search the Deleted Items folder—you might consider emptying it before you commence this search in order to save time and reduce confusion in the results.

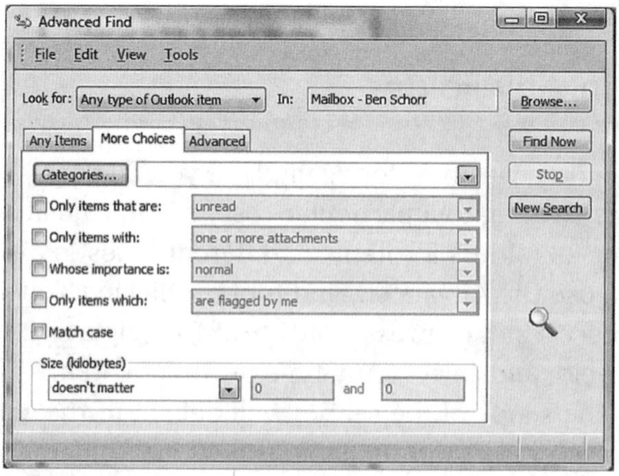

FIGURE 12.12

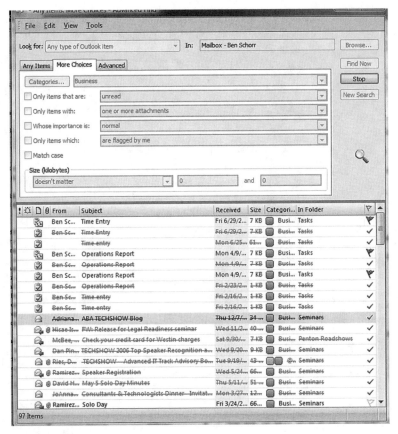

FIGURE 12.13

Summary

Outlook has some powerful tricks that you can use to be even more productive, from easy ways to calculate future dates to ways to keep useful features useful by removing extraneous or incorrect information. Don't be afraid to customize Outlook with useful views or to open multiple windows so that you can more effectively work with your data. Becoming an Outlook power user is not just fun at parties, it also can help you be better at your job and more effective in life.

Keyboard Shortcuts to Make You Smile 13

If you're a fast typist, you may prefer to use keyboard shortcuts to achieve things in Outlook rather than taking your hands off the keyboard to use the mouse. Luckily, just about anything you can do with the mouse you can also do with the keyboard. In this chapter we'll take a look at how to successfully use Outlook from the keyboard.

Create New Items

You can create any kind of new Outlook item from any Outlook folder. To create a new item in the current folder just press CTRL+N. Whatever kind of folder it is, that's what kind of item will be created (Figure 13.1). Here's how to create items:

- New Mail Message (CTRL+SHIFT+M)
- New Appointment Item (CTRL+SHIFT+A)
- New Contact (CTRL+SHIFT+C)
- New Task (CTRL+SHIFT+K)
- New Journal Entry (CTRL+SHIFT+J)
- New Note (CTRL+SHIFT+N)

You can also create a new Folder (CTRL+SHIFT+E) or new Search Folder (CTRL+SHIFT+P) from the keyboard at any time.

📄	Mail Message	Ctrl+N
📨	Post in This Folder	Ctrl+Shift+S
📁	Folder...	Ctrl+Shift+E
🔍	Search Folder...	Ctrl+Shift+P
	Navigation Pane Shortcut...	
📅	Appointment	Ctrl+Shift+A
📅	Meeting Request	Ctrl+Shift+Q
📇	Contact	Ctrl+Shift+C
👥	Distribution List	Ctrl+Shift+L
📋	Task	Ctrl+Shift+K
📋	Task Request	Ctrl+Shift+U
📓	Journal Entry	Ctrl+Shift+J
📝	Note	Ctrl+Shift+N
📠	Internet Fax	Ctrl+Shift+X
📑	Choose Form...	
📑	Choose InfoPath Form...	Ctrl+Shift+T
	Outlook Data File...	

FIGURE 13.1

Working with Existing Items

Some keyboard shortcuts for working with existing items are old news.
ALT+R (or CTRL+R if you prefer) to Reply to the selected message, ALT+W
(or CTRL+F, curiously enough) to Forward the selected message, and of
course DELETE to delete the selected message. Some of you may vaguely
remember such shortcuts as CTRL+P to print the selected message or
CTRL+SHIFT+R to Reply to All. Others are not as obvious but very handy
nonetheless—for instance, if you want to set the follow-up flag options
on a selected message, press CTRL+SHIFT+G. You may want to highlight
that sentence—if you're using the follow-up flag as often as you should be,
you'll want to use that shortcut quite a bit. CTRL+SHIFT+V is a great way
to move the selected message to a subfolder (Figure 13.2).

When you're editing an e-mail message, you're using the Word editor, so all of the Word keyboard shortcuts work (things like CTRL+B for

FIGURE 13.2

bold, CTRL+E to center, etc.), but so do the old Outlook shortcuts like CTRL+Enter to send your e-mail message when you're done. Be careful with that one—on a few occasions I've accidentally pressed CTRL+Enter or ALT+S and sent the e-mail message prematurely, a potentially embarrassing error.

Perhaps the most useful keyboard shortcut for working with existing items is CTRL+A, which selects all of the items in the view. This is especially handy when you want to do something with all of the items in a folder, be it move them all, delete them all, print them all, or whatnot.

Navigate Outlook

You can also navigate the program using the keyboard. The Go menu shows the available shortcuts (Figure 13.3).

- Go to Mail Folder (CTRL+1)
- Go to Calendar Folder (CTRL+2)
- Go to Contacts (CTRL+3)
- Go to Tasks (CTRL+4)
- Go to the Folder List (CTRL+6)
- Go to Journal (CTRL+8)

FIGURE 13.3

Want to go to a folder not on that list? Press CTRL+Y to get the "Go to Folder" dialog box pictured in Figure 13.4. From there, you can use the arrow keys on your keyboard to navigate up or down the list, or just start typing the name of the folder you want. This will work great *except* if the folder you want is a subfolder of a folder that is not expanded, in which case starting to type the name of the folder won't do any good. If you have a lot of folders and know the path to the folder you want, you can press ALT+F to get to the Folder Name field at the top of the dialog box and type the path to the folder as in "clients\Joe Smith" (without the quotes), and you'll be taken to that folder right away. Naturally, the downside to that technique is that you have to know the exact name, complete path, and correct spelling of the folder you want.

FIGURE 13.4

Do you have a message item open and you want to just go to the next message without closing the message item and having to select the next item manually? Press CTRL+period (CTRL+.) to view the next message. Press CTRL+comma (CTRL+,) to view the previous message.

Want something a little more advanced? If you're in a folder and want to move between the Navigation Pane and the other elements of the window such as the To-Do Bar, press F6 to move left to right and SHIFT+F6 to move right to left. That's great for the real hardcore keyboard folks; though I have to admit that I rarely use it myself. Some of you may be thinking that you can use TAB and SHIFT+TAB to do the same thing, and you actually can, *but* . . . TAB and SHIFT+TAB are actually more granular. They will take you to the smaller sub-windows within the main folder elements. TAB relates to F6 the way a local train relates to an Express. TAB is going to stop at every little window, such as the search box and the calendar and task elements of the To Do Bar, while F6 is only going to stop at each of the major elements like (in the case of mail) the Navigation Pane, Message List, Reading Pane, and the Tasks section of the To-Do Bar.

Tricks of the Pros

You're probably familiar with the "Back" button (and to a lesser extent the "Forward" button) from your Internet browser as a way to go back to (or forward to) a previously viewed Web page. Outlook actually respects the same concept—using Back (and Forward) to take you to previously viewed folders or views. Want to quickly go back to the last folder you were looking at in Outlook? Press ALT+Left Arrow. Try it, it's cool.

Of course if you're looking to go to the Search Box in Outlook, the fastest way is to just press F3. That will take you directly to the Search Box.

Insert Things into an Item

While you're editing an Outlook item you can use the keyboard to insert various elements into the item.

- Date and Time (ALT+SHIFT+F)
- Hyperlink (CTRL+K)

Also the usual Windows Cut (CTRL+X), Copy (CTRL+C) and Paste (CTRL+V) keyboard shortcuts will work just fine.

Searching

As I mentioned previously, if you want to go straight to the Search Box, you can just press F3. So you've gone to the Search Box and conducted your search. Didn't find what you want? You can immediately convert your search to an All Folders (whatever kind of folder it is—mail, calendar, etc.) search for the same string by pressing CTRL+ALT+A. Found what you wanted and want to just clear your search? Press ESC.

> **From the Department of "Cool!"**
>
> When you run a search and you press CTRL+ALT+K, your search will be run against all of the files on your computer.

If you want to do a somewhat more sophisticated search, you can press CTRL+ALT+W to expand the Search Query Builder (Figure 13.5), which gives you more options than just the basic Search Box. And no, you don't already have to be in the Search Box to do that. It will work from wherever you are in the program. Press CTRL+ALT+W again to turn the Search Query Builder back off. Need to run an even more powerful search? CTRL+SHIFT+F will launch the Advanced Find tool, which is probably familiar to those of you who used it in Outlook 2003 and earlier versions.

FIGURE 13.5

If you have a message open and you want to search for text within it, press F4 to open that search box.

Summary

Fast typists sometimes resent having to take their hands off the keyboard to use the mouse. Outlook gives you many ways to use the program without ever touching the mouse. From navigation to searching to creating new content—you can do it all without ever needing to think about your mouse.

Index

The Lawyer's Guide to Marketing Your Practice, Second Edition

Edited by James A. Durham and Deborah McMurray
This book is packed with practical ideas, innovative strategies, useful checklists, and sample marketing and action plans to help you implement a successful, multi-faceted, and profit-enhancing marketing plan for your firm. Organized into four sections, this illuminating resource covers: Developing Your Approach; Enhancing Your Image; Implementing Marketing Strategies and Maintaining Your Program. Appendix materials include an instructive primer on market research to inform you on research methodologies that support the marketing of legal services. The accompanying CD-ROM contains a wealth of checklists, plans, and other sample reports, questionnaires, and templates—all designed to make implementing your marketing strategy as easy as possible!

The 2008 Solo and Small Firm Legal Technology Guide

By Sharon D. Nelson, John Simek, and Michael C. Maschke
This annual guide is the only one of its kind written to help solo and small firm lawyers find the best legal technology for their dollar. You'll find the most current information and recommendations on computers, servers, networking equipment, legal software, printers, security products, smartphones, and anything else a law office might need. It's written in plain language to make implementation easier if you choose to do it yourself--or you can use it in conjunction with your IT consultant. Either way, you'll learn how to make technology work for you.

The Lawyer's Guide to Strategic Planning: Defining, Setting, and Achieving Your Firm's Goals

By Thomas C. Grella and Michael L. Hudkins
This practice-building resource is your guide to planning dynamic strategic plans and implementing them at your firm. You'll learn about the actual planning process and how to establish goals in key planning areas such as law firm governance, competition, opening a new office, financial management, technology, marketing and competitive intelligence, client development and retention, and more. The accompanying CD-ROM contains a wealth of policies, statements, and other sample documents. If you're serious about improving the way your firm works, increasing productivity, making better decisions, and setting your firm on the right course, this book is the resource you need.

The Successful Lawyer: Powerful Strategies for Transforming Your Practice

By Gerald A. Riskin
Available as a Book, Audio-CD Set, or Combination Package.
Global management consultant and trusted advisor to many of the world's largest law firms, Gerry Riskin goes beyond simple concept or theory and delivers a book packed with practical advice that you can implement right away. By using the principles found in this book, you can live out your dreams, embrace success, and awaken your firm to its full potential. Large law firm or small, managing partners and associates in every area of practice—all can benefit from the information contained in this book. With this book, you can attract what you need and desire into your life, get more satisfaction from your practice and your clients, and do so in a systematic, achievable way.

How to Start and Build a Law Practice, Platinum Fifth Edition

By Jay G Foonberg
This classic ABA bestseller has been used by tens of thousands of lawyers as the comprehensive guide to planning, launching, and growing a successful practice. It's packed with over 600 pages of guidance on identifying the right location, finding clients, setting fees, managing your office, maintaining an ethical and responsible practice, maximizing available resources, upholding your standards, and much more. You'll find the information you need to successfully launch your practice, run it at maximum efficiency, and avoid potential pitfalls along the way. If you're committed to starting—and growing—your own practice, this one book will give you the expert advice you need to make it succeed for years to come.

Flying Solo: A Survival Guide for Solo and Small Firm Lawyers, Fourth Edition

Edited by K. William Gibson
This fourth edition of this comprehensive guide includes practical information gathered from a wide range of contributors, including successful solo practitioners, law firm consultants, state and local bar practice management advisors, and law school professors. This classic ABA book first walks you through a step-by-step analysis of the decision to start a solo practice, including choosing a practice focus. It then provides tools to help you with financial issues including banking and billing; operations issues such as staffing and office location and design decisions; technology for the small law office; and marketing and client relations. Whether you're thinking of going solo, new to the solo life, or a seasoned practitioner, *Flying Solo* provides time-tested answers to real-life questions.

ABA LawPracticeManagementSection
MARKETING · MANAGEMENT · TECHNOLOGY · FINANCE

30-Day Risk-Free Order Form
Call Today! 1-800-285-2221
Monday–Friday, 7:30 AM – 5:30 PM, Central Time

Qty	Title	LPM Price	Regular Price	Total
_____	The Lawyer's Guide to Collaboration Tools and Technologies: Smart Ways to Work Together (5110589)	$59.95	$ 89.95	$_____
_____	The Lawyer's Guide to Marketing on the Internet, Third Edition (5110585)	74.95	84.95	$_____
_____	The Lawyer's Field Guide to Effective Business Development (5110578)	49.95	59.95	$_____
_____	The Electronic Evidence and Discovery Handbook: Forms, Checklists, and Guidelines (5110569)	99.95	129.95	$_____
_____	The Lawyer's Guide to Adobe® Acrobat, Third Edition (5110588)	49.95	79.95	$_____
_____	The Law Firm Associate's Guide to Personal Marketing and Selling Skills (5110582)	39.95	49.95	$_____
_____	Trainer's Manual for the Law Firm Associate's Guide to Personal Marketing and Selling Skills (5110581)	49.95	59.95	$_____
_____	The Lawyer's Guide to Marketing Your Practice, Second Edition (5110500)	79.95	89.95	$_____
_____	The 2008 Solo and Small Firm Legal Technology Guide (5110657P)	49.95	79.95	$_____
_____	The Lawyer's Guide to Strategic Planning (5110520)	59.95	79.95	$_____
_____	The Successful Lawyer: Powerful Strategies for Transforming Your Practice (5110531)	64.95	84.95	$_____
_____	How to Start and Build a Law Practice, Platinum Fifth Edition (5110508)	57.95	69.95	$_____
_____	Flying Solo: A Survival Guide for Solo and Small Firm Lawyers, Fourth Edition (5110527)	79.95	99.95	$_____

*Postage and Handling	
$10.00 to $24.99	$5.95
$25.00 to $49.99	$9.95
$50.00 to $99.99	$12.95
$100.00 to $349.99	$17.95
$350 to $499.99	$24.95

**Tax
DC residents add 5.75%
IL residents add 9.00%

*Postage and Handling	$_____
**Tax	$_____
TOTAL	$_____

PAYMENT

❑ Check enclosed (to the ABA)

❑ Visa   ❑ MasterCard   ❑ American Express

_____
Account Number   Exp. Date   Signature

Name _____ Firm _____

Address _____

City _____ State _____ Zip _____

Phone Number _____ E-Mail Address _____

Guarantee
If—for any reason—you are not satisfied with your purchase, you may
return it within 30 days of receipt for a complete refund of the price of the
book(s). No questions asked!

Mail: ABA Publication Orders, P.O. Box 10892, Chicago, Illinois 60610-0892
♦ **Phone: 1-800-285-2221** ♦ **FAX: 312-988-5568**

E-Mail: abasvcctr@abanet.org ♦ **Internet: http://www.lawpractice.org/catalog**